Ubuntu Leadership: Transforming Business Through the Power of African Principles

Redefining Leadership through

through

Community, Culture, and

Collaboration

Avhurengwi Nengovhela

Introduction

What if the most effective leadership practices in today's globalized world were not born in the boardrooms of New York or London, but rather in the communal circles of Africa, where community and consensus reign supreme? This provocative question invites us to rethink longstanding assumptions about leadership. For many business leaders and managers, students and scholars, as well as entrepreneurs and small business owners, there's a growing curiosity about how diverse cultural perspectives can enhance leadership effectiveness. Particularly enticing is the exploration of non-Western methodologies, such as those inspired by rich African heritage and the principles embedded within it.

Consider the vibrant scene of a bustling marketplace in Accra, Ghana. Here, the laughter of children intertwines with the rhythmic calls of vendors, each hoping to catch the attention of passersby. Every sale is much more than a commercial exchange; it is a reflection of the deeply entrenched community spirit, a reminder that interactions in leadership mirror these daily exchanges—rooted in connection, trust, and mutual support. In these moments, one discovers that leadership does not exist in isolation but is intricately woven into the fabric of community life.

Traditional leadership paradigms often focus on individual achievement, competitive edge, and top-down directives. However, what if the concepts of Ubuntu and communalism from African societies offered transformative insights for today's organizations? Ubuntu, an idea encapsulated by the phrase "I am because we are," stresses interdependence and collective unity, challenging the notion that successful leadership solely revolves around individual merit and hierarchical power.

Studies reveal that organizations led by community-focused leaders report a 30% increase in employee engagement and satisfaction. Yet, these benefits remain underappreciated in mainstream corporate settings. This statistic underscores a significant opportunity: while many companies grapple with issues like employee disengagement and high turnover rates, they could benefit from adopting African leadership models prioritizing community acknowledgment and shared success.

The relevance of African leadership principles extends far beyond the continent's boundaries, finding applicability across various sectors worldwide. As global challenges evolve, the complexity and uncertainty require innovative approaches to leadership. The principles of Ubuntu and communalism offer potent strategies for cultivating resilience and fostering innovation—attributes increasingly crucial in navigating modern organizational landscapes.

Business leaders focused on elevating their influence should recognize the potential of these principles. Imagine company environments where empathy and solidarity form the backbone of management strategies, bridging gaps between team members and dismantling silos that hinder collaboration. Implementing communal leadership practices reshapes organizational culture, instilling a sense of belonging and purpose among employees, ultimately driving sustainable success.

Similarly, students and academics stand to gain from delving into the intersection of African heritage and contemporary leadership theories. By exploring diverse narratives and examining alternative frameworks, academic pursuits can uncover new pathways for understanding global leadership dynamics. This enriches curriculum content and equips future leaders with the knowledge required to navigate multicultural contexts effectively.

For entrepreneurs and small business owners, these insights herald fresh opportunities to foster a team-centric culture, essential for growth and stability. Embracing community values can prove invaluable, enabling businesses to cultivate loyalty and adapt to changing market demands. In essence, African-inspired leadership not only enhances internal cohesion but also builds bridges with external customers and partners, ensuring long-term viability.

In a world characterized by rapid technological advancements and profound cultural shifts, traditional leadership approaches may no longer suffice. Organizations must be agile, adaptable, and empathetic to meet evolving needs. African leadership principles respond to this call for change, offering a blueprint for leading authentically in complex environments. Adoption requires an openness to shift away from conventional practices and embrace broader perspectives inherited from diverse cultures.

By applying these philosophies, leaders embark on a transformational journey, marked by heightened awareness and sensitivity to the interconnectedness of human experiences. The result is a reconceptualization of leadership as an inclusive practice centered around nurturing human potential and reinforcing relationships rather than perpetuating divisive tactics.

Leaders who successfully integrate African principles into their strategic arsenal can differentiate themselves in an era demanding authenticity, compassion, and vision. They possess the tools to inspire through example, forging bonds based on trust and loyalty. Furthermore, they manifest optimism amid adversity, guiding their teams toward meaningful outcomes aligned with universal values.

Thus, the invitation remains open: as you embark on your journey through the pages of this book, consider the possibility that profound lessons await discovery in unexpected places. Engage deeply with stories of African leadership, allowing them to broaden your horizons and reshape your understanding of what defines true leadership. Together, let's unlock the potential of incorporating community-oriented methodologies into the wider conversation on leadership excellence.

In weaving collective wisdom into the fabric of our organizational structures, we invite an enriched dialogue where empathy and unity become cornerstones of contemporary leadership. By daring to look beyond familiar borders and conventional wisdom, we create space for innovation and transformation that informs the future generations of leaders—a legacy cemented in shared achievement, guided by the enduring principles of humane leadership.

The Essence of African Leadership

African leadership is a multifaceted tapestry woven from historical experiences and evolving cultural practices, profoundly influencing contemporary governance across the continent. In this chapter, we explore how these rich traditions and values play a crucial role in shaping leadership models today. By delving into past leadership styles, we aim to uncover the enduring principles that have guided communities through generations. These insights not only reflect African societies' unique approaches to leadership but also offer invaluable lessons for modern leaders seeking to enhance their effectiveness by integrating cultural perspectives beyond Western paradigms.

Throughout this chapter, readers will journey through the historical contexts that shaped African leadership, starting from pre-colonial times when kinship and community were integral to decision-making processes. We will examine the impacts of colonial interruptions on leadership practices and the subsequent adaptations that have emerged. The discussion also highlights post-colonial efforts to blend traditional values with modern governance, emphasizing the ongoing relevance of consensus-building, communalism, and Ubuntu as foundational elements. Additionally, this chapter presents an analysis of how globalization has influenced hybrid leadership models, showcasing examples from various African nations where traditional principles are harmonized with contemporary demands. This exploration provides a comprehensive understanding of how African leadership continues to evolve, offering practical guidance for those looking to foster team-centric cultures and leverage community values in today's global landscape.

Historical Context and Evolution of African Leadership

African leadership is deeply rooted in its historical evolution, a journey that unfolds through various intricate phases. Pre-colonial Africa exhibited leadership structures that were intrinsically linked to kinship and communal ties, laying a foundation of accountability and collective decision-making. Leaders emerged not from a pursuit of power but through a selection process grounded in trust and responsibility towards the community. This system emphasized the value of interconnectedness, where decisions were made with a focus on the welfare of the entire community. For instance, tribal elders often held significant influence due to their wisdom and perceived fairness, guiding the community in reaching consensual agreements.

The advent of colonialism brought seismic shifts in these traditional systems. Colonial powers imposed hierarchical structures that disrupted these indigenous practices, instigating an era of resistance and adaptation. African societies, accustomed to more egalitarian and participatory governance, found themselves grappling with imposed foreign authority, often leading to conflicts and upheavals. The imposition altered the socio-political landscape, birthing new post-colonial leadership models. These movements sought to reclaim autonomy and redefine leadership in a way that resonated more closely with pre-colonial values, while simultaneously addressing the challenges posed by the colonial legacy.

Post-colonial Africa was characterized by a struggle to blend traditional leadership traits with modern governance structures. Here, it becomes essential to offer guidelines for understanding how traditional values could inform contemporary leadership. One such guideline involves recognizing the importance of consensus-building as a tool for fostering unity and commitment among diverse groups within the society. This practice not only honors the past but also enhances democratic processes by ensuring decisions reflect the will of the people.

In recent decades, the movement towards democracy has highlighted principles of accountability and transparency. Democratic governance in Africa aims to reconcile ancient traditions of collective responsibility with the demands of modern governance. This transition emphasizes open dialogue and inclusivity, reflecting the desires of the populace in governmental affairs. As African nations evolve, they strive to balance respect for cultural heritage with the implementation of systems that foster responsible leadership, thereby creating a robust framework for governance that promotes both growth and stability.

Globalization further enriches this narrative by introducing hybrid leadership models that interweave local traditions with global influences. This trend has resulted in unique leadership landscapes across the continent, where traditional African values coexist with contemporary global practices. For example, business leaders might incorporate communal decision-making into their strategies while adopting technological innovations that boost efficiency and competitiveness. A guideline here would be to encourage leaders to cultivate a blend of local cultural insights with global management philosophies, thus creating a dynamic approach to leadership that celebrates diversity while embracing innovation.

Illustrative examples abound; South Africa's transition to a democratic society under Nelson Mandela is a prime instance of reconciling traditional African leadership values with modern democratic ideals. Mandela's leadership style, which emphasized reconciliation and forgiveness, drew heavily from African traditions of ubuntu—a term embodying humanity and compassion. Likewise, Rwanda's post-genocide recovery showcases a leadership model that blends traditional conflict resolution methods with modern governance tactics, fostering national healing and sustainable development.

As African societies navigate this complex interplay of past and present, an appreciation for the historical context is crucial. Understanding the impact of colonial interruptions and the resilient adaptations made by African communities provides valuable lessons for today's leaders. It is through this lens that contemporary African leadership continues to evolve, seeking paths that honor ancestral wisdom while meeting the demands of a rapidly changing world.

To fully appreciate the trajectory of African leadership, one must engage with both its historical roots and current transformations. By exploring the nuances of pre-colonial, colonial, and post-colonial eras, we gain insight into the enduring influence of cultural heritage on leadership styles. Modern leaders can glean valuable lessons from this rich tapestry, using it as a guide to foster inclusive and effective leadership practices that resonate with African values while participating actively on the global stage.

Core Values and Comparative Analysis of African vs. Western Leadership

In understanding African leadership, it's essential to embrace the values and philosophies that have shaped its practices across generations. One of these foundational principles is Ubuntu, a philosophy deeply embedded in African cultural heritage. Ubuntu conveys a deep sense of interconnectedness among individuals, emphasizing compassion, respect, and the prioritization of collective goals over individual ambitions. This philosophy teaches that "I am because we are," highlighting our intrinsic connection to one another. In leadership, this perspective fosters environments where leaders prioritize the wellbeing of their community, encouraging unity and mutual respect.

Ubuntu serves as a guiding light for leaders, advocating for decisions that reflect communal welfare. For instance, a leader underpinned by Ubuntu values might focus on initiatives that uplift entire communities rather than projects benefiting a select few. This approach nurtures trust and loyalty, as people recognize that their leader genuinely values everyone's input and wellbeing. Such inclusivity and regard for collective interests often lead to robust support systems within organizations and communities, promoting both social harmony and organizational success.

Similarly, communalism plays a critical role in shaping African leadership. This value emphasizes community-driven decision-making processes, where every voice is not only heard but also valued. Unlike hierarchical models common in Western paradigms, where decisions are often top-down, African communalism champions participation from all members of society. Leaders adopting this model benefit from diverse perspectives, leading to more comprehensive and culturally sensitive solutions. By fostering collaboration and shared responsibility, communalism helps build resilient teams that can adapt to challenges and innovate creatively.

Consensus-building is another pivotal element of African leadership practices. It ensures that decisions are born from dialogue and mutual agreement, rather than authoritative decrees. This method strengthens commitment to collective decisions as everyone feels a part of the process, ensuring seamless implementation and adherence. In settings where differing opinions are prevalent, consensus-building facilitates an inclusive environment, minimizing conflict and promoting peaceful coexistence. It stands as a testament to the power of patience and empathy in leadership, encouraging leaders to seek middle ground for the greater good.

However, implementing consensus-building methods requires specific strategies to ensure effectiveness. First, it's crucial to establish open platforms where dialogues can flourish without fear of judgment or retribution. Leaders should encourage transparency and honesty, inviting participants to share their views freely. Facilitators must be adept at navigating discussions to counter biases and mediate conflicts, ensuring every opinion is considered before reaching a decision. Moreover, cultivating environments of respect and trust is necessary so that even dissenting voices feel valued and understood.

Comparing African collectivism with Western individualism reveals intriguing contrasts in leadership styles. While Western paradigms often emphasize personal achievements and competition, African models lean towards shared accountability and cohesive teamwork. In practice, this means valuing the group's success over individual gains, which can lead to more sustainable and inclusive growth. For example, in a business setting, while Western leaders might reward top performers individually, African-inspired leadership would celebrate team accomplishments, encouraging members to learn from each other and grow collectively.

The strengths of African collectivism become particularly evident in times of crisis or when innovation is needed. A team-centric approach ensures that resources and skills are pooled, leading to creative problem-solving and resilience. This stands in contrast to models driven by individual excellence, where isolated efforts might fail to address complex problems effectively. By nurturing an environment that values collaboration, leaders can inspire groundbreaking ideas and foster a culture of continuous improvement.

Leadership influenced by African values also tends to favor flat organizational structures over rigid hierarchies commonly found in Western contexts. In such setups, decision-making authority is distributed more evenly, empowering individuals at all levels to contribute meaningfully. These environments thrive on trust and mentorship, allowing knowledge and skills to flow freely between members. However, transitioning to flatter structures may require guidelines to balance autonomy with accountability. Regular feedback loops and transparent communication channels can help maintain clarity and ensure objectives align with organizational goals.

Cultural sensitivity is another significant consideration for those exploring diverse leadership methodologies. By understanding the cultural dynamics at play, leaders can better navigate cross-cultural interactions and tailor their strategies to various socio-cultural contexts. Leaders must develop cultural competence, showing respect and appreciation for divergent traditions and practices. This sensitivity fosters respectful collaborations and strengthens relationships across different cultures, paving the way for inclusive environments where diversity is leveraged for mutual benefit.

Insights and Implications

As we conclude our exploration of African leadership, it becomes evident that the profound values and historical contexts greatly influence contemporary practices. The chapter has illuminated how pre-colonial structures, with their roots in kinship and communal ties, laid a foundation emphasizing accountability and collective decision-making. Even as colonial disruptions introduced hierarchical models that shifted traditional systems, these earlier principles continue to inform and guide modern leadership approaches. By understanding the enduring significance of consensus-building, interconnectedness, and collective responsibility, leaders today are better equipped to foster an inclusive environment reflective of these timeless ideals.

In bridging the gap between ancestral wisdom and present-day demands, modern African leadership offers unique insights for navigating complex sociopolitical landscapes. As we have seen through examples like South Africa's democratic transition and Rwanda's post-genocide recovery, integrating traditional values such as Ubuntu into governance can drive societal harmony and sustainable development. For business leaders and entrepreneurs, these lessons highlight the potential of cultivating trust, collaboration, and cultural awareness within organizations. By celebrating diversity and embracing both local and global influences, today's leaders can craft dynamic approaches to leadership that not only resonate with African heritage but also contribute significantly to global discourse on effective management practices.

Reference List

20th WCP: Ubuntu: An African Assessment of the Religious Other. (n.d.). Www.bu.edu. https://www.bu.edu/wcp/Papers/Afri/AfriLouw.htm

Igboin, B. O. (2016). *Traditional leadership and corruption in pre-colonial Africa: how the past affects the present*. Studia Historiae Ecclesiasticae (SHE). https://doi.org/10.17159/2412-4265/2016/228

Lutz, D. W. (2009). *African "Ubuntu" Philosophy and Global Management*. Journal of Business Ethics. https://www.jstor.org/stable/27749670

Muiu, M. wa. (2010). *Colonial and Postcolonial State and Development in Africa*. Social Research. https://www.jstor.org/stable/23347128

Community-Centric

Leadership

Community-centric leadership is a dynamic approach that places the community at the heart of decision-making processes. This leadership style recognizes the immense value of engaging with diverse community voices, fostering an environment where inclusivity and collaboration thrive. The foundation of community-centric leadership rests on the principles of drawing from collective intelligence, valuing varied perspectives, and integrating these insights into strategic planning. By creating spaces for community involvement, leaders can unlock innovative solutions that reflect the true needs and aspirations of the people they serve. This introduction sets the stage for exploring how leaders can build trusted alliances by aligning organizational strategies with community values.

This chapter delves into the transformative impact of incorporating community-focused leadership within organizations. It highlights how such approaches not only enhance collaboration and trust but also promote accountability among stakeholders. Readers will uncover methods for implementing collaborative decision-making models that empower communities and ensure equitable participation. Additionally, the chapter examines the role of cultural sensitivity in decision-making, emphasizing the importance of respecting local norms and values to foster deeper connections. Through a narrative lens, the chapter further explores the establishment of robust feedback mechanisms, ensuring transparent communication and adaptability. Readers will gain insights into how aligning organizational goals with community priorities enhances credibility and nurtures sustainable growth. Ultimately, this chapter provides actionable guidance for leaders seeking to harness the potential of community-centric approaches, offering pathways to meaningful engagement and shared success.

Community's Role in Decision-Making

In community-centric leadership, involving the community in decision-making processes yields more inclusive and effective outcomes. Businesses stand to gain significantly when they engage community stakeholders, drawing from the collective intelligence and varied perspectives that such involvement brings. Inclusivity is at the heart of this approach; it broadens the decision-making process by incorporating diverse views, thereby leading to more comprehensive and well-rounded solutions.

Engaging with a variety of community stakeholders can enhance inclusivity by tapping into different experiences and backgrounds. When businesses actively seek out these diverse perspectives, they foster an environment where people feel valued and included, ultimately nurturing a sense of belonging within both the organization and the community. This diversity not only pulls in fresh ideas but also mitigates blind spots that could hinder the effectiveness of organizational strategies. By recognizing the value each stakeholder brings to the table, leaders can make decisions that are more reflective of collective needs and aspirations, setting the stage for sustainable growth and development.

To effectively harness these diverse viewpoints, organizations can implement collaborative decision-making models. These models serve as a framework for integrating multiple voices and ideas, encouraging innovative solutions that align organizational goals with community needs. Such models empower communities by valuing their input and embedding their insights into strategic planning processes. For instance, participatory decision-making fosters a cooperative atmosphere where the exchange of ideas thrives. Leaders utilizing these models can bridge gaps between varying priorities, ensuring that the resulting decisions are not only innovative but also grounded in the realities and expectations of the community.

Collaborative decision-making models go beyond mere participation; they require an active commitment to dialogue and consensus-building. A key guideline for implementing these models successfully involves structuring decision-making sessions to encourage balanced contributions from all stakeholders. This often means setting clear agendas, facilitating open discussions, and creating mechanisms for equitable participation. Such structures help prevent dominant voices from overshadowing others, ensuring that all perspectives are fairly represented and considered. Furthermore, using tools like online forums or workshops can engage participants who might otherwise be excluded due to geographical or social barriers, thus promoting wider inclusion.

Understanding cultural practices in decision-making further enriches community engagement by acknowledging and appreciating the cultural significance that influences stakeholder perspectives. By aligning decision-making processes with local values, organizations enhance their credibility and reputation within the community. This cultural sensitivity fosters deeper connections and commitments from community members, who see their traditions and values respected and integrated into the decision-making process. It becomes crucial for leaders to be culturally literate, which involves recognizing and adapting to the specific cultural norms and practices that can impact stakeholder engagement and decision acceptance.

A guideline for integrating cultural practices into decision-making includes conducting cultural assessments to identify relevant customs, practices, and attitudes within the community. Leaders should invest time in understanding these cultural factors and designing decision-making frameworks that resonate with them. By doing so, they not only respect cultural nuances but also leverage them to create processes that are meaningful and inspiring for all involved.

Feedback mechanisms play a critical role in maintaining ongoing community input, serving as a foundation for transparent communication and adaptability. Establishing robust feedback channels allows organizations to remain attuned to the evolving needs and concerns of the community. By actively seeking and responding to feedback, leaders demonstrate a commitment to continuous improvement and accountability, enhancing their credibility within the community.

One essential guideline for establishing effective feedback mechanisms is to ensure they are accessible and representative. This can involve using multiple platforms, such as surveys, focus groups, and digital forums, to capture a broad spectrum of community voices. Transparency is another key component, requiring leaders to clearly communicate how feedback will be used and to provide updates on actions taken in response to community input. Such openness builds trust and reinforces the organization's dedication to working collaboratively with its stakeholders.

Trust and Responsibility in Community-Centric Leadership

In the intricate dance of leadership, community-centric approaches offer a harmonizing rhythm that fosters trust and shared accountability—two pillars essential for organizational success. By embracing transparency in operations, leaders can cultivate a loyal workforce while also forming strong alliances with community partners.

Transparency, at its core, involves open communication about strategies, decisions, and challenges. When leaders engage transparently, they effectively remove the cloak of secrecy that often breeds distrust and disengagement. This openness invites employees to partake in a journey where they are well-informed about both triumphs and trials. For instance, sharing quarterly financial results or strategic shifts ensures that employees and community partners alike understand the organization's trajectory. Clarity in these communications not only maintains trust but also encourages loyalty. Studies suggest that when employees feel included in their organization's narrative, their engagement levels soar, ultimately paving the path for long-lasting partnerships (Eisenberger & Stinglhamber, 2011).

Moreover, consistent engagement with stakeholders serves as the bridge to fortifying trust further. Proactive outreach coupled with active listening forms the cornerstone of this engagement. Leaders who regularly connect with stakeholders, be it through town hall meetings, surveys, or informal check-ins, showcase a commitment to understanding and addressing concerns. These interactions should not merely be transactional; instead, they ought to foster a dialogue that allows stakeholders to voice their thoughts and opinions. In doing so, leaders not only strengthen ties but also demonstrate a genuine appreciation for diverse perspectives. This is crucial, as engagement underlines the importance of an inclusive culture where every stakeholder feels heard and valued, thus deepening the foundations of trust.

Aligning organizational values with community norms is another avenue through which community-centric leadership carves its niche. When organizations mirror the values held dear by their communities, it enhances credibility and promotes collaborative problem-solving. For example, a company operating in a region prioritizing environmental conservation might adopt green practices not just as a compliance measure but as a core value. Such alignment signals respect for community priorities and sends a powerful message of solidarity. It creates an environment where shared beliefs drive collective action, turning potential challenges into opportunities for innovation and growth.

Recognizing contributions within a collective framework also plays a pivotal role in encouraging mutual responsibility. Systems of accountability should be designed not to assign blame, but to highlight achievements and areas for improvement. Celebrating victories, regardless of scale, reinforces positive behavior and instills a sense of pride among contributors. Furthermore, acknowledging the efforts of teams rather than individuals underscores the idea of collective success, fostering a mindset where accountability is shared. This structure invites teams to learn from setbacks and strive for continuous improvement, knowing that their contributions are valued within the broader organizational tapestry.

Importantly, establishing accountability systems that resonate with community-centric values ensures everyone understands their role in the overarching mission. These systems must be transparent and equitable, allowing for constructive feedback and growth. When employees perceive accountability as fair and balanced, they are more likely to take ownership of their responsibilities and remain committed to the organization's goals.

Final Insights

The chapter has explored how community-focused leadership can enhance collaboration, trust, and accountability by integrating diverse perspectives in decision-making processes. By involving the community in these decisions, leaders tap into a wealth of knowledge and experiences that result in more inclusive and effective outcomes. This approach fosters a sense of belonging among stakeholders, ensuring that varied voices contribute to the shaping of organizational strategies. Through collaborative models, organizations not only harness innovative solutions but also align their goals with the broader aspirations of the communities they serve.

Additionally, establishing transparent communication and feedback mechanisms is crucial in sustaining this engagement and maintaining trust within the community. By actively listening and responding to feedback, leaders demonstrate an ongoing commitment to improvement and accountability. Cultural sensitivity further enriches this process by aligning organizational practices with local norms, thereby reinforcing credibility and fostering deeper connections. Ultimately, this chapter underscores the importance of blending transparency, inclusivity, and cultural respect in creating leadership frameworks that not only reflect collective values but also drive sustainable growth and mutual responsibility.

Reference List

Canavesi, A., & Minelli, E. (2021). *Servant Leadership and Employee Engagement: a Qualitative Study.* Employee Responsibilities and Rights Journal.

Hadziahmetovic, N., & Salihovic, N. (2022, June 17). *The Role of Transparent Communication and Leadership in Employee Engagement.* ResearchGate; Human Resource Management Academic Research Society. https://www.researchgate.net/publication/362053309_The_Role_of_Transparent_Communication_and_Leadership_in_Employee_Engagement

Rodrigues, S. (2022, April 20). *5 Reasons to Include Community in Decision-Making | ThoughtExchange.* Thought Exchange. https://thoughtexchange.com/blog/5-reasons-to-include-community-in-decision-making/

Thomas, T. (2024, April 30). *Three Strategies to Increase Community Engagement Inclusion.* PublicInput. https://publicinput.com/wp/3-strategies-to-increase-community-engagement-inclusion/

Integrating Cultural Intelligence

Integrating cultural intelligence is a pivotal aspect of developing successful leadership strategies in today's diverse organizational landscapes. It entails understanding and respecting different cultural perspectives, which ultimately strengthens team dynamics and fosters an inclusive environment. Cultural intelligence is not just a skill but a mindset that leaders need to cultivate by recognizing the profound impact of cultural diversity on communication, decision-making, and collaboration. By leveraging cultural insights, leaders can enhance their effectiveness and create workplaces where everyone feels valued and understood.

This chapter delves into practical approaches for integrating cultural intelligence within organizations. It emphasizes recognizing and adapting to diverse cultural frameworks, helping leaders navigate complexities with more sensitivity and awareness. The discussion explores how cultural dimensions like Power Distance and Individualism shape interactions and influence leadership styles. Readers will uncover strategies for identifying and mitigating cultural biases, ensuring equitable decision-making processes. Additionally, this chapter highlights the significance of assessing organizational culture through tools like employee surveys and the benefits such assessments offer in aligning cultural integration efforts. Furthermore, it underscores the importance of cultural awareness training in equipping leaders with the necessary tools to navigate cross-cultural situations adeptly. By exploring these key areas, the chapter provides valuable insights into crafting a culturally intelligent approach tailored to modern leadership challenges, addressing the distinct needs of business leaders, academics, and entrepreneurs alike.

Recognizing and Adapting to Diverse Cultural Frameworks

Recognizing and adapting to various cultural frameworks is a pivotal skill for leaders aiming to maximize their effectiveness in diverse settings. By appreciating different cultural dimensions, as illustrated by Geert Hofstede's framework, leaders can gain profound insights into how values vary across cultures, impacting team interactions and attitudes toward authority and social norms. Hofstede's model highlights six key cultural dimensions: Power Distance, Individualism vs. Collectivism, Masculinity vs. Femininity, Uncertainty Avoidance, Long-Term vs. Short-Term Orientation, and Indulgence vs. Restraint. Each dimension offers a lens through which leaders can better understand the cultural underpinnings that influence behaviors within organizations.

To illustrate, consider the Power Distance dimension, which examines the extent of acceptance by less powerful members in society regarding unequal power distribution. In high power distance cultures, hierarchical structures are deeply ingrained, requiring leaders to ensure all voices are heard, even from those at lower levels. Conversely, in low power distance societies, fostering egalitarianism may be more appropriate. This understanding helps leaders tailor their approaches, ensuring inclusive participation and engagement from all team members.

Identifying cultural biases is another crucial component of effective leadership. Leaders must engage in continuous self-reflection to recognize preconceived notions that may unconsciously shape their decision-making processes. Cultural biases often stem from deeply embedded stereotypes or assumptions about other groups that leaders might not be aware of. By confronting these biases, leaders can create a more equitable decision-making environment. A practical example of addressing cultural bias could involve workshops where leaders actively explore their cultural preconceptions and discuss strategies to mitigate their impacts on organizational decisions.

An assessment of organizational culture is essential for leaders seeking to align cultural integration strategies with existing dynamics. Conducting employee surveys serves as a valuable tool in gauging the current cultural landscape within an organization. These surveys can uncover perceptions, attitudes, and feelings towards the prevailing culture, offering invaluable insights into potential areas for improvement. Once leaders have a clear understanding of the cultural dynamics at play, they can devise strategies to harmoniously integrate diverse cultural perspectives, promoting a cohesive work environment.

Value of cultural awareness training cannot be overstated in its role of enhancing empathy and equipping leaders with the necessary tools to navigate complex cultural interactions. Such training programs often include simulations, workshops, and interactive modules designed to immerse leaders in different cultural experiences. By exposing leaders to scenarios that require them to think and act outside their cultural comfort zones, cultural awareness training fosters a deeper understanding and appreciation for diverse cultural norms and practices. This not only enhances empathy but also prepares leaders to handle multicultural interactions with sensitivity and insight.

Incorporating these key strategies into leadership development involves recognizing and adapting to various cultural frameworks, understanding cultural dimensions, identifying biases, assessing organizational culture, and valuing cultural awareness training. By focusing on these aspects, leaders cultivate environments that embrace diversity, foster inclusivity, and leverage cultural strengths for improved organizational performance.

Moreover, integrating technology can further enhance leaders' ability to engage with cultural complexity. Digital tools, such as mobile apps that offer cultural etiquette tips and language translation software, assist in facilitating smoother multicultural communications. For instance, sentiment analysis AI can help managers interpret unspoken emotions, adding an empathetic layer to their leadership approach. Incorporating technological advancements elevates leaders' cultural intelligence, thereby strengthening team cohesion and collaboration.

Encouraging Adaptive Leadership and Cross-Cultural Collaboration

Integrating cultural intelligence in leadership means developing strategies for adaptive leadership and fostering cross-cultural collaboration. In today's globalized world, understanding the unique tapestry of diverse cultures within an organization is a vital component of effective leadership. Flexible leadership approaches are crucial as they allow leaders to adjust tactics to fit various cultural contexts and elevate team engagement.

Leaders who embrace flexibility are better equipped to navigate the complexities of cultural differences and leverage them to enhance their leadership effectiveness. This adaptability involves being open to new ideas, reevaluating one's assumptions, and modifying strategies to align with the cultural values and expectations of team members. For instance, in cultures that prioritize collective decision-making, a leader might need to shift from a more directive approach to one that emphasizes consensus-building. This not only fosters a sense of inclusion but also enhances team cohesion and productivity.

The success of adaptive leadership can be seen in numerous case studies where leaders have adopted flexible strategies within multicultural environments. These leaders often demonstrate an ability to synthesize different cultural insights into actionable strategies. One practical example might involve a manager who leads a team spread across multiple countries; this leader understands the importance of local market expertise and tailors communication styles accordingly. By appreciating and utilizing the distinct capabilities each team member brings from their cultural background, these leaders ensure that decisions reflect a comprehensive understanding of their operating environment.

Fostering open communication is another essential strategy in enhancing cross-cultural collaboration. Transparent dialogue prevents misjudgments and helps build trust, which is foundational when working within diverse teams. Encouraging open discussions about expectations, deadlines, and responsibilities ensures that all team members feel heard and valued. Moreover, leaders should set channels for continuous feedback and address any misunderstandings promptly. For example, regular team check-ins and culturally sensitive conflict resolution meetings can significantly reduce potential friction within a team. These practices promote a culture where team members are comfortable expressing their perspectives, thus contributing to more innovative solutions and efficient problem-solving.

Celebrating cultural diversity actively acknowledges the varied backgrounds within a team and uses this acknowledgment to strengthen team bonding and inclusivity. Organizing events that highlight cultural differences is an effective way to cultivate an inclusive workplace atmosphere. Such events could include cultural appreciation days where team members share elements from their heritage, whether through food, music, or storytelling. Celebrations such as these do not only foster mutual respect but also instill a sense of belonging among team members. When individuals see their culture being respected and celebrated, it enhances their connection to the organization and boosts morale.

Incorporating guidelines for these strategies aids in creating an organized approach for leaders looking to implement cultural intelligence effectively. First, leaders should assess the cultural makeup of their teams and identify areas where flexible leadership can make a significant difference. Adopting flexible leadership isn't merely about accommodating differences but strategically leveraging diverse talents for organizational goals. Leaders should aim to balance different cultural expectations with the organization's objectives to create a harmonious work environment.

Furthermore, guidelines on fostering open communication require leaders to establish clear communication protocols that are accessible to all team members, regardless of their cultural backgrounds. This includes training in cultural sensitivity and active listening to ensure that all voices are recognized and respected. On celebrating cultural diversity, it's beneficial for organizations to develop a calendar of events that recognizes major cultural festivals represented within their teams, encouraging participation and learning opportunities.

Adaptive leadership is integral to navigating the cultural diversity present in modern workplaces. It requires a willingness to learn continuously and evolve, embracing a mindset that sees cultural differences as strengths rather than challenges. The strategies highlighted—adopting flexible leadership approaches, examining successful case studies, fostering open communication, and celebrating cultural diversity—are pivotal in building a strong, cohesive, and culturally intelligent team.

Insights and Implications

In this chapter, we explored the vital role of cultural insights in shaping effective leadership within diverse organizations. By recognizing and adapting to various cultural frameworks, leaders can significantly enhance their understanding of team dynamics and interactions. Key strategies include familiarizing with Hofstede's cultural dimensions, identifying and addressing cultural biases, and conducting thorough assessments of organizational culture to align integration strategies accordingly. Such awareness equips leaders to tailor their approaches to fit the unique cultural contexts of their teams, fostering an inclusive environment where every member feels valued. The importance of cultural awareness training was highlighted as a means to develop deeper empathy and navigate multicultural settings with sensitivity. Moreover, leveraging technology provides additional support by improving communication and raising leaders' cultural intelligence.

The chapter further underscores the significance of adaptive leadership and cross-cultural collaboration as integral components of modern leadership practices. Effective leaders are those who embrace flexibility and facilitate open communication to build trust within diverse teams. By celebrating cultural diversity through shared experiences and perspectives, leaders encourage stronger team bonds and inclusivity. Practical guidelines offer actionable steps for integrating these insights, such as adopting flexible leadership strategies, encouraging transparent dialogue, and organizing cultural events. These efforts not only help leaders harness the strengths of diverse cultural backgrounds but also promote a cohesive and innovative team culture. Overall, the chapter emphasizes that appreciating and utilizing cultural diversity can drive enhanced organizational performance and foster sustainable growth.

Reference List

Cultural Competency | Effective Team Management. (n.d.). Hackinghrlab.io. https://hackinghrlab.io/blogs/cultural-competency-training-managers/

Deloitte. (2023). *Working in multicultural teams |Deloitte Australia | Diversity, Inclusion and Leadership consulting case study.* Www.deloitte.com. https://www.deloitte.com/au/en/services/consulting/perspectives/working-multicultural-teams.html

Ireland, in. (2024, October 4). *Effective Leadership & Inclusive Solutions using Coaching, Development & Consulting in Ireland, Uk & Europe.* Effective Leadership & Inclusive Solutions Using Coaching, Development &

Consulting in Ireland, Uk & Europe.
https://www.silewalsh.com/leadership-blog/how-hofstedes-cultural-dimensions-framework-supports-inclusive-leadership

Yukl, G., & Mahsud, R. (2010). *Why Flexible and Adaptive Leadership Is Essential*. ResearchGate.
https://www.researchgate.net/publication/232567495_Why_flexible_and_adaptive_leadership_is_essential

Harnessing Traditional

Wisdom

Harnessing traditional wisdom involves uncovering the rich tapestry of knowledge embedded in African traditions, particularly their application in modern leadership and organizational culture. This chapter delves into how centuries-old practices rooted in storytelling and community-centric conflict resolution can provide fresh insights for contemporary leaders seeking to foster cohesion and innovation within their teams. Such wisdom is not only a repository of historical narratives but also a vital source of ethical guidance and communal values essential for today's organizational landscapes. As businesses navigate increasingly complex cultural dynamics, embracing these age-old traditions offers pathways to create more inclusive, resilient, and culturally sensitive environments.

Within this exploration, the chapter examines the intricate role of oral traditions in leadership, highlighting how stories transcend mere entertainment to become powerful tools for connection and motivation. Leaders who effectively weave storytelling into their communication strategies can inspire teams, align them with overarching goals, and build a shared sense of purpose. By integrating narratives that resonate on personal and cultural levels, organizations can cultivate a unique collective identity that strengthens teamwork and drives sustained success. Moreover, the chapter explores indigenous conflict resolution methods, offering a window into approaches that prioritize healing and reconciliation over confrontation. These principles, when adapted thoughtfully, hold transformative potential for resolving workplace disputes and enhancing overall group harmony. Whether through the artful telling of stories or the empathetic practices of mediation, the insights garnered from traditional African systems promise to enrich both leadership effectiveness and organizational culture in profound ways.

Utilizing Oral Traditions in Leadership

Oral traditions and storytelling hold a deep-rooted significance in leadership, offering a profound connection between communal wisdom and modern organizational practices. At the heart of this tradition is the transmission of wisdom and community values, which serves to enhance organizational narratives. Oral traditions are not merely stories told through generations; they encapsulate culture, societal norms, and collective memory. Within African communities, for example, storytelling is an art form that preserves history and guides decision-making processes. By integrating these narratives into leadership, organizations can develop a richer narrative that resonates with team members on a personal and cultural level, fostering a deeper understanding of shared goals and values.

One of the most compelling aspects of storytelling in leadership is its ability to strengthen emotional bonds within teams, consequently improving goal alignment. Stories have an unparalleled power to connect people emotionally and intellectually. Leaders who harness storytelling can convey complex ideas in ways that engage and inspire their audiences. A well-told story captures attention, evokes emotion, and drives action. In a business environment, this translates to better communication, where messages are delivered with clarity and impact. When leaders use stories that reflect the team's collective experiences and aspirations, they create a sense of belonging and purpose, aligning the entire organization towards common objectives. This emotional connection is vital for motivating individuals and teams to work collaboratively towards achieving strategic goals.

Moreover, cultivating storytelling fosters inclusivity by allowing diverse voices to be heard. Oral traditions, by nature, encourage participation from various segments of a community, particularly those whose perspectives are often marginalized. In the corporate realm, the inclusion of diverse stories ensures that different viewpoints are acknowledged and respected.

This diversity of thought enriches the organization's culture, leading to more innovative solutions and strategies. By valuing and incorporating stories from employees at all levels, leaders demonstrate a commitment to inclusivity, empowering individuals to express their unique contributions to the company's mission.

Leaders can also leverage oral traditions to articulate vision and bridge generational divides. Storytelling offers a narrative structure that conveys a leader's vision compellingly and memorably. Through stories, leaders can illustrate potential futures, outline paths to success, and explain how everyone plays a part in realizing organizational objectives. Additionally, oral traditions provide a bridge between generations, as they encompass timeless themes and lessons that resonate across ages. In environments where multiple generations collaborate, such as businesses with veteran and millennial employees, this storytelling approach helps build a cohesive culture. It encourages understanding and respect for each generation's distinct values and experiences, creating a harmonious workplace where knowledge flows freely and innovation thrives.

A practical guideline for leaders seeking to integrate storytelling effectively is to ensure authenticity and relatability. Stories should be genuine reflections of the organization's ethos and employee experiences. Leaders might consider workshops or storytelling sessions where team members share personal and professional anecdotes that align with organizational objectives. This not only builds camaraderie but also provides a repository of relatable content for future storytelling endeavors.

Incorporating Indigenous Conflict Resolution Methods

In the realm of contemporary leadership and organizational culture, there is a growing recognition of the value embedded in traditional African knowledge systems. A critical component of such wisdom lies in indigenous conflict resolution practices that offer fresh perspectives on effective problem-solving. By examining these age-old methods, we can unearth valuable insights that address modern challenges within various organizational settings.

One of the most compelling features of indigenous conflict resolution is its community-centric approach. This method champions collective outcomes over punitive measures, prioritizing the well-being of the community above individual grievances. Unlike some Western judicial systems that focus heavily on assigning guilt and administering punishment, indigenous practices often emphasize reconciliation and healing. This approach fosters an environment where members work together towards common goals, enhancing group cohesion and unity. In organizations, adopting this mindset can build robust teams that thrive on collaboration rather than competition, ultimately boosting overall productivity and morale.

Within these frameworks, restorative justice techniques play a significant role. Practices such as mediation are integral, designed to foster empathy and trust among the parties involved. Mediation allows conflicting parties to engage in dialogue, encouraging each participant to express their feelings and perspectives. This process nurtures mutual understanding and strengthens relationships by transforming conflict into an opportunity for growth and development. As individuals share their stories and listen to one another, they develop empathetic bonds that extend beyond mere resolution, solidifying trust and elicit lasting peace. For leaders aiming to cultivate compassionate work environments, embedding restorative justice principles into their problem-solving strategies can yield transformative results.

A prime example of these principles in action is Rwanda's Gacaca courts. These community-driven solutions emerged in the aftermath of the Rwandan genocide as a means of addressing the vast number of cases the conventional legal system could not handle efficiently. The Gacaca system empowered local communities to play a direct role in the justice process, emphasizing the importance of truth-telling, repentance, and forgiveness. Community members were invited to participate in the hearings, contributing to the decision-making process and ensuring that the outcomes resonated with local customs and values. This grassroots approach provided victims and perpetrators an opportunity to rebuild relationships and restore social harmony. Organizations inspired by this model can facilitate holistic recovery through inclusive decision-making processes that respect and utilize the diverse voices within their teams.

An essential facet of integrating these practices into modern leadership lies in training leaders in traditional conflict resolution techniques. Equipping leaders with these skills empowers them to handle disputes constructively, drawing on time-tested methodologies that prioritize cooperation and mutual respect. Training programs can incorporate simulations and role-playing exercises to immerse leaders in scenarios that require employing indigenous strategies. These experiences provide valuable practical knowledge that enhances their ability to manage conflicts proactively, reducing potential workplace disruptions.

As organizations increasingly operate within multicultural settings, embracing diverse conflict resolution methods contributes to inclusive and adaptable cultures. When leaders harness the collective wisdom encapsulated in traditional practices, they not only enrich their problem-solving arsenal but also promote a spirit of inclusivity that resonates throughout the organization. Furthermore, incorporating these approaches signals respect for cultural traditions, reinforcing organizational commitment to diversity and cultural sensitivity.

While many aspects of indigenous conflict resolution offer intrinsic value, applying these approaches within organizations requires careful adaptation. Practical strategies entail fostering open communication channels that encourage feedback and dialogue at all levels. Leaders should create safe spaces for discussion where employees feel valued and heard, facilitating constructive conversations even during challenging times. Additionally, establishing mentorship programs that pair experienced leaders with those newer to the field can help disseminate these practices throughout the organization effectively.

For business leaders, managers, and entrepreneurs, understanding and implementing these indigenous practices can lead to enhanced leadership effectiveness and team cohesion. By acknowledging the relevance of traditional African wisdom, organizations can transcend cultural boundaries and build environments that leverage community values for sustainable growth. As students and academics explore the intersection of African heritage and contemporary leadership theories, these insights provide rich material for study and application.

Bringing It All Together

In this chapter, we delved into the rich tapestry of traditional African knowledge systems and their transformative impact on modern leadership and organizational culture. The insights gained from oral traditions and indigenous practices reveal how these age-old wisdoms foster stronger emotional bonds within teams, enhance communication, and promote inclusivity. By leveraging storytelling in leadership, organizations can create narratives that resonate with employees' cultural backgrounds, ensuring everyone feels valued and understood. Additionally, incorporating indigenous conflict resolution methods offers fresh perspectives on addressing challenges, emphasizing community-centric approaches that prioritize reconciliation over punishment. These practices not only resolve conflicts effectively but also nurture empathy and trust among team members, building a cohesive work environment.

Understanding and integrating these traditional methods empower leaders to bridge cultural divides, fostering a spirit of unity across diverse teams. As we've explored, embracing such practices enriches problem-solving strategies and nurtures a sense of belonging and purpose. For business leaders, managers, and entrepreneurs, applying these insights can lead to enhanced leadership effectiveness and a thriving organizational culture. Similarly, for students and academics, unraveling the intersection of African heritage and contemporary leadership theories offers deep insights into global leadership paradigms. As organizations recognize the value of these traditional knowledge systems, they are uniquely positioned to transcend cultural boundaries, creating sustainable workplaces grounded in respect and community values.

Reference List

Milwaukee Public Museum. (n.d.). *Oral Tradition | Milwaukee Public Museum*. Www.mpm.edu. https://www.mpm.edu/content/wirp/ICW-14

Mogomotsi, P. K., Mogomotsi, Goemeone E.J, & Hambira, Wame L. (2020). *An Institutional Economic Analysis*. Africa Development / Afrique et Développement; CODESRIA; JSTOR. https://www.jstor.org/stable/26936566

Palmer, N. (2015, April 15). *Inside the Gacaca Courts*. Oxford University Press EBooks; Oxford University Press. https://doi.org/10.1093/acprof:oso/9780199398195.003.0005

Valdez, C. (2024, March 19). *The Importance of Indigenous Oral Traditional Storytelling: Part 2 |*

Cultural Survival. Www.culturalsurvival.org.
https://www.culturalsurvival.org/news/importance-indigenous-oral-traditional-storytelling-part-2

Building Sustainable Organizations

Building sustainable organizations is a significant undertaking that requires a holistic perspective and keen insight into cultural dynamics. African leadership principles offer a unique lens through which businesses can navigate the complexities of sustainability. By engaging with the values and practices inherent in these traditions, organizations can gain fresh perspectives that often challenge conventional Western management practices. This chapter delves into how African leadership philosophies, rooted in communal wisdom and collective decision-making, can transform modern organizational environments. These traditional values not only foster resilience but also align organizations more closely with their social environments, contributing to sustainable development goals. Readers will discover how these ancient insights provide businesses with tools to adapt to modern challenges while remaining culturally relevant and community-focused.

The following chapter explores several key themes central to building sustainable organizations. It examines the role of indigenous wisdom in shaping long-term vision and strategic planning within organizations. The narrative highlights traditional activities such as storytelling and communal decision-making as pivotal elements that foster innovation and align business strategies with community values. Furthermore, the discussion extends to participatory decision-making processes that emphasize inclusivity, thereby strengthening stakeholder commitment and organizational stability. Noteworthy examples underscore how aligning organizational objectives with community aspirations contributes to mutual growth and trust. Continuous learning emerges as a crucial aspect of sustainable growth, where experiential learning and adaptability are emphasized. Throughout this chapter, readers will encounter case studies that illustrate the successful integration of traditional practices with contemporary advancements, offering practical insights for business leaders, scholars, and entrepreneurs seeking to enhance their leadership capabilities and organizational effectiveness.

Strategies for Long-Term Vision and Planning

An African perspective on long-term visioning can profoundly impact the sustainability of organizations by drawing upon rich cultural traditions and integrating them into modern management practices. One key aspect is the incorporation of indigenous wisdom, which entails tapping into centuries-old knowledge systems to address contemporary challenges. This approach often leads to solutions that are both innovative and culturally relevant, ensuring they resonate well with local communities. Traditional practices such as storytelling, communal decision-making, and land stewardship provide a framework for creating business strategies that align closely with community values. By leveraging these ancestral insights, organizations can develop unique approaches that foster deep connections with their social environment.

A critical pillar in African leadership philosophy is participatory decision-making. Engaging all stakeholders in the organizational planning process is not merely an optional strategy but an essential one. This inclusive approach ensures diverse voices are heard and considered, which actively fosters a strong sense of ownership and commitment among team members and the broader community. When people feel that they have a say in the direction and decisions of an organization, their dedication to its success naturally increases. This participation extends beyond internal stakeholders to include external entities like local governments, tribal leaders, and community representatives. The result is a collaborative network committed to shared goals, enhancing stability and adaptability in uncertain times.

The alignment of organizational goals with the ambitions of the community it serves forms another vital element of sustainable practice. In many African societies, the concept of Ubuntu—emphasizing human interconnectedness and mutual support—plays a crucial role. Organizations that integrate these principles prioritize community welfare alongside corporate growth. This alignment strengthens the social contract between the organization and its surroundings, creating a mutually beneficial relationship. By aligning their objectives with those of the community, businesses can ensure that their operations contribute positively to local development, enhancing trust and cooperation.

Continuous learning is another cornerstone of sustainable organizational growth. Embracing a culture of ongoing improvement allows organizations to remain agile and responsive in a rapidly changing global landscape. African leadership strategies often emphasize experiential learning, adaptability, and resilience, essential traits for long-term success. Encouraging employees to engage in regular training, skill development, and feedback loops helps cultivate an environment where innovation thrives. This culture of continuous enhancement not only supports sustainable growth but also boosts employee morale and retention, ensuring that the organization remains competitive and forward-thinking.

To illustrate these concepts further, consider a case where an organization implements indigenous agricultural techniques alongside modern methods to increase crop yields sustainably. By partnering with local elders knowledgeable in traditional farming practices, the organization capitalizes on historical success while introducing new technologies. Decisions regarding planting cycles, resource allocation, and harvesting schedules are made collaboratively with community input, ensuring that all stakeholders have a vested interest in the outcomes. Furthermore, the company's initiatives are designed to coincide with local educational programs, providing training opportunities that promote lifelong learning. Such efforts demonstrate the powerful synergy between respecting cultural heritage and pursuing contemporary advancements.

Balancing Economic Growth with Social Responsibilities

In today's rapidly evolving business landscape, striking a balance between profitability and social responsibility is paramount. Embracing corporate social responsibility (CSR) is no longer just a moral choice, but a strategic imperative. Integrating CSR into business models ensures that companies generate profit while positively impacting society.

Businesses should start by aligning their values with social goals, ensuring that CSR becomes an intrinsic part of their organizational DNA. Developing such models requires understanding that economic gain and societal benefits can complement each other. Companies like TOMS have demonstrated that integrating social causes into their brand identity not only generates goodwill but also drives profitability and long-term success.

Transparent communication is at the heart of successful CSR strategies. It involves creating channels where stakeholders can engage in meaningful dialogues about the company's social initiatives. Establishing transparency builds trust and credibility. When stakeholders, including customers, employees, and investors, are aware of the efforts and impact of a company's CSR activities, the results often include increased loyalty and support. For instance, businesses that openly discuss their environmental policies tend to attract environmentally conscious consumers who value this openness and commitment to sustainability.

Measuring impact and maintaining accountability are critical components in the realm of CSR. Companies must establish clear metrics to assess the success of their initiatives. These measurements should encompass both qualitative and quantitative data. For example, firms can track reductions in carbon emissions or improvements in local community conditions due to their interventions. Measurement helps ensure that CSR efforts are not only symbolic gestures but deliver real-world outcomes.

Accountability involves regular audits and reporting, providing insights into the effectiveness of CSR actions. This transparency doesn't just satisfy ethical considerations; it aligns with the increasing demand from consumers and regulators for businesses to disclose their environmental, social, and governance (ESG) data. With rigorous evaluation, organizations can continually refine their strategies, ensuring that social objectives align with business goals.

Partnering with local organizations offers a powerful avenue for amplifying social impact. Collaboration with grassroots entities provides companies with unique insights into community needs and cultural nuances. By working closely with local partners, businesses can develop tailored initiatives that directly address pressing issues, enhancing the relevance and acceptance of their efforts.

Local partnerships pave the way for shared value creation, which benefits both communities and corporations. For example, a multinational corporation might collaborate with a local NGO to improve educational facilities, thereby empowering future generations and cultivating a skilled workforce. In these scenarios, the synergy between global resources and local knowledge creates a win-win situation that strengthens both the business and social fabric of the community.

Summary and Reflections

Leadership is a multifaceted journey that evolves by embracing diverse perspectives, and the principles of African leadership offer profound insights into nurturing resilient and sustainable organizations. By integrating indigenous wisdom, organizations can draw upon centuries-old cultural traditions to navigate modern challenges effectively. This chapter highlights how practices such as storytelling, communal decision-making, and land stewardship can serve as frameworks for developing strategies aligned with community values. Engaging all stakeholders in participatory decision-making ensures their voices are valued, fostering a strong sense of ownership and commitment. Such inclusive approaches encourage deeper connections with both internal team members and external partners, including local governments and community representatives. These methods advance stability, adaptability, and mutual trust between organizations and the communities they serve.

Moreover, aligning organizational goals with community ambitions, a cornerstone emphasized in African philosophies like Ubuntu, ensures that operations benefit everyone involved. The concept underscores human interconnectedness and mutual support, highlighting the importance of placing community welfare alongside corporate growth. Moreover, an ongoing commitment to continuous learning and improvement fuels sustainable growth and innovation, ensuring organizations remain agile in a rapidly evolving landscape. By embracing experiential learning and adaptability, organizations not only boost employee morale but also enhance their competitiveness. Through these thoughtful integrations of African leadership principles, businesses craft unique paths that resonate deeply with their social environments, cultivating a foundation for enduring success and shared progress.

Reference List

Bwalya Chibwe, Terry, N., Koffi Dodji Noumonvi, Liam Carpenter-Urquhart, Sènankpon Tcheton, & Pereira, L. (2024, January 1). *African futures: a review of scenarios for Indigenous and local people and nature in Africa.* Ecology and Society; Resilience Alliance. https://doi.org/10.5751/es-15322-290332

Ganti, A. (2024, June 12). *Social responsibility in business: Meaning, types, examples, and criticism.* Investopedia. https://www.investopedia.com/terms/s/socialresponsibility.asp

Ketprapakorn, N., & Kantabutra, S. (2022, July). *Toward an organizational theory of sustainability culture.* Sustainable Production and Consumption. https://doi.org/10.1016/j.spc.2022.05.020

Murphy, C. (2024, January 27). *Why is social responsibility important to a business?* Investopedia. https://www.investopedia.com/ask/answers/041015/why-social-responsibility-important-business.asp

Challenges to Adoption

Adopting African leadership principles worldwide presents a unique set of challenges, rooted in deep-seated cultural misconceptions and integration hurdles. These difficulties often arise from stereotypes that misrepresent African leadership, painting it with broad strokes as inherently ineffective or autocratic. Such views ignore the fundamental aspects of communal participation and shared responsibilities that define many traditional African leadership models. The reluctance to embrace these principles globally could be attributed to a misunderstanding of their values, such as Ubuntu, which emphasizes unity and collective welfare. This resistance overlooks the potential benefits that adopting such inclusive practices can bring, particularly in terms of fostering environments conducive to collaboration and personal growth. Therefore, breaking down these barriers requires a careful examination and appreciation of the rich array of leadership practices that have emerged from African cultures over centuries.

This chapter explores the multifaceted obstacles to embracing African leadership methods beyond the continent. Readers will delve into the prevalent cultural stereotypes that obscure the true essence of African leadership values and practices. By addressing these misconceptions, we aim to highlight how principles like consensus-building and interconnectedness can be effectively woven into various organizational frameworks. Additionally, the discussion encompasses the challenges of ethical adoption without crossing into cultural appropriation, underscoring the importance of genuine learning and adaptation. Business leaders, academics, and entrepreneurs will find guidance on navigating the complexities of integrating these non-Western methodologies within their structures. Furthermore, the text outlines strategies for overcoming organizational inertia and skepticism, emphasizing the role of leadership commitment, training, and feedback mechanisms in easing transitions. Through this understanding, the chapter provides a roadmap for readers interested in leveraging the strengths of African leadership principles to create more inclusive, collaborative, and resilient organizations.

Cultural Misconceptions and Integration Challenges

African leadership has often been misunderstood, primarily due to the prevalence of stereotypes that cast it in a negative light. These stereotypes frequently depict African leadership as synonymous with dictatorship and inefficiency. However, this perspective overlooks the rich communal and participatory dimensions that are intrinsic to many African leadership models. For instance, leadership in many African communities is deeply rooted in collective decision-making and shared responsibilities. This collaborative approach can be seen throughout history, from traditional village councils to modern corporate boardrooms where community-focused strategies are employed. By focusing primarily on negative imagery, people miss out on the opportunity to learn from these inclusive practices that emphasize unity, consensus, and a shared vision for progress.

Another area of misunderstanding lies in the values that underpin African leadership, such as Ubuntu. Ubuntu, which translates to "I am because we are," emphasizes interconnectedness and community welfare. Despite its powerful message of inclusivity and resilience, many remain hesitant to embrace it due to misconceptions about its applicability in competitive environments. Yet, businesses across the globe could benefit from incorporating Ubuntu's principles by fostering environments that support collective growth and personal development. Companies that have adopted Ubuntu-inspired initiatives have seen improvements in employee satisfaction and collaboration, thus challenging the narrative that such values are irrelevant or outdated in modern settings.

Skepticism also surrounds communal decision-making practices prevalent in African leadership frameworks. Critics often question the efficiency of involving multiple stakeholders in the decision-making process, assuming it delays action and stifles innovation. However, what these critiques fail to recognize is how communal decision-making can lead to stronger buy-in and enhanced accountability. When individuals within an organization feel their voices are heard and valued, they are more likely to commit to the organization's goals. This inclusive approach not only builds trust but also ensures decisions are well-rounded and reflect the diverse perspectives within the group.

A critical aspect when adopting or integrating elements of African leadership into other contexts is avoiding cultural appropriation. The line between cultural appropriation and appreciation is often blurred in practice, leading to misunderstandings and even exploitation. Cultural appropriation involves the unacknowledged or inappropriate adoption of elements from one culture by individuals of another, particularly when those doing the adopting belong to a dominant culture. It is essential for business leaders and organizations to distinguish between appropriation and appreciation in order to promote respectful engagement and successful integration. This requires a conscious effort to understand the significance behind specific leadership practices and values, acknowledging their origins and intended purposes. According to Cruz et al. (2023), recognizing power dynamics and historical context is paramount in ensuring cultural exchanges are conducted ethically and respectfully.

Practically, businesses aiming to incorporate African leadership principles should engage in cultural appreciation through genuine learning and adaptation rather than superficial mimicking. This means investing time and resources in understanding the cultural nuances that inform these leadership styles. Leaders can attend workshops, read literature authored by African thought leaders, and collaborate with experts in African leadership philosophies. By doing so, they show respect and dedication to understanding the core essence of these cultures, thereby creating authentic applications within their organizations.

Moreover, setting guidelines for ethical cultural exchange is crucial for preventing appropriation. Engaging with cultural representatives to guide adaptations can provide insight and authenticity, ensuring the practices serve their original purposes while being applicable in new contexts. Establishing partnerships and collaborations with African leaders and communities also creates a mutually beneficial relationship that honors and respects cultural heritage.

Organizational Resistance to Change

Organizational resistance to adopting new leadership styles is a significant challenge that many companies face. As global businesses increasingly turn to non-Western models, including African leadership principles, understanding how to overcome internal resistance becomes crucial for successful implementation. One of the key elements in addressing this challenge is establishing psychological safety within the organization. Employees need to feel secure in expressing their thoughts and concerns during transitions. This sense of safety fosters trust between employees and management, which is essential for performance improvement. Trust allows team members to voice innovative ideas without fear of negative consequences, encouraging a culture of openness and collaboration.

Leadership commitment plays an indispensable role in overcoming resistance to change. Leaders who demonstrate a thorough commitment to new practices can effectively counter inertia, which often hinders progress. By embodying the values they wish to instill, leaders can inspire their teams to embrace changes actively. Committed leaders serve as role models, showcasing the benefits of adopting novel leadership methods and motivating others to follow suit. This dedication is particularly important when implementing unfamiliar practices that may initially appear daunting.

Moreover, training and development programs are critical in easing organizational transitions to new leadership styles. Education helps dispel fears and misconceptions associated with these changes. Providing comprehensive training enables employees to understand the rationale behind the new methods and equips them with the necessary skills to adapt. Such programs should focus not only on the mechanics of the new practices but also on the cultural and philosophical underpinnings, which are often integral to non-Western leadership styles. For instance, understanding the communal and participatory aspects of African leadership can help employees appreciate its potential benefits in fostering inclusivity and resilience, both at individual and organizational levels.

Feedback mechanisms are another vital component in managing resistance to change. Implementing effective feedback systems allows organizations to continually assess and refine their strategies. These mechanisms enable employees to express their views about the transition process and provide insights into potential improvements. Regular feedback helps identify areas of concern early, allowing leaders to make timely adjustments. It also reassures employees that their opinions matter, thus enhancing their engagement and driving continuous improvement. Organizations should aim to create an environment where feedback is not only sought but also valued and acted upon.

Summary and Reflections

The chapter explored the barriers to the global adoption of African leadership principles, focusing on cultural misconceptions and organizational resistance. Through examining these challenges, it became evident that stereotypes often overshadow the unique attributes of African leadership, such as its communal and participatory nature. Misunderstandings about values like Ubuntu further exacerbate hesitancy towards integration, despite their potential benefits in fostering inclusivity and resilience. The narrative highlighted that incorporating African principles requires a genuine appreciation of cultural nuances and conscious efforts to distinguish between appropriation and appreciation. Business leaders are encouraged to engage in thoughtful learning and adaptation, ensuring respectful and effective application within their organizations.

Additionally, the chapter addressed how overcoming organizational resistance is essential for integrating new leadership styles. Establishing psychological safety and demonstrating leadership commitment emerged as pivotal factors in facilitating acceptance of change. Training programs play a crucial role in educating employees about non-Western leadership models, providing them with skills to embrace new practices. Implementing feedback mechanisms further supports the transition by allowing continuous evaluation and improvement. These strategies collectively underscore the importance of understanding both the philosophical and practical aspects of African leadership, paving the way for successful adoption and fostering a culture of collaboration and growth.

Reference List

Appelbaum, S., Medea Cesar Degbe, Macdonald, O., & Thai-Son Nguyen-Quang. (2015, March 2). *Organizational outcomes of leadership style and resistance to change (Part One)*. ResearchGate; Emerald. https://www.researchgate.net/publication/27335285 7_Organizational_outcomes_of_leadership_style_an d_resistance_to_change_Part_One

Cruz, A. G. B., Seo, Y., & Scaraboto, D. (2023, April 3). *Between Cultural Appreciation and Cultural Appropriation: Self-Authorizing the Consumption of Cultural Difference* (L. L. Price, M. Giesler, & H. J. Schau, Eds.). Journal of Consumer Research. https://doi.org/10.1093/jcr/ucad022

Khaw, K. W., Alnoor, A., Abrrow, H. A. -, Tiberius, V., Ganesan, Y., & Atshan, N. A. (2022). *Reactions towards organizational change: A systematic literature review*. Current Psychology; Springer. https://doi.org/10.1007/s12144-022-03070-6

Nicholas, G. (2018, October 5). *Confronting the Specter of Appropriation*. SAPIENS. https://www.sapiens.org/culture/cultural-appropriation-halloween/

Case Studies of Success

Examining successful implementations of African leadership practices in global businesses reveals a transformative potential harnessing tradition and modernity. Leadership driven by principles deeply embedded in community values and cultural norms creates powerful synergies, merging the old with the new to address contemporary challenges. In a world where organizations are continuously seeking innovative leadership strategies, these practices stand out for their effectiveness and global applicability. They offer unique frameworks that prioritize inclusivity, mentorship, and cultural specificity, establishing pathways for sustainable growth and prosperous business environments.

This chapter delves into several real-world examples highlighting how African leadership principles have been woven into diverse organizational settings, achieving remarkable results. It showcases various sectors—from commodities trading and tech startups to multinational corporations and NGOs—illustrating the multifaceted applications of community-oriented decision-making and generational mentorship. Through detailed case studies, readers will gain insights into trust-building strategies that bolster profitability, innovation accelerated by traditional knowledge transfer, and community-led initiatives enhancing program delivery and volunteer participation. Additionally, the integration of communal values into corporate cultures is explored, demonstrating how such practices lead to increased employee satisfaction and retention. By examining these stories, the chapter aims to inspire business leaders, students, and entrepreneurs to embrace and adapt these proven strategies within their own endeavors, fostering environments of shared success and collective advancement.

Real-world Examples and Their Outcomes

In today's globally connected world, businesses are seeking innovative leadership strategies that go beyond the conventional norms. African leadership practices, deeply rooted in community and tradition, are proving to be effective and transformative in various sectors worldwide. This subpoint highlights organizations successfully integrating these principles into their operational frameworks, yielding impressive outcomes.

One notable case is that of African Commodity Traders. These enterprises have demonstrated how community-oriented decision-making can bolster profitability. By prioritizing trust-building within local communities and markets, these traders have not only increased their market share but have also enhanced overall business sustainability. The strategy focuses on engaging stakeholders at every level, ensuring that decisions reflect communal interests and values. Such an approach has strengthened relationships with suppliers and buyers, establishing a network of trust that supports long-term growth.

Another remarkable example comes from a Local Tech Start-up, which has accelerated innovation and shortened product development timelines by embracing mentorship grounded in African traditions. In many African cultures, knowledge transfer occurs through generational mentorship, where elders pass down wisdom and skills to younger members of the community. By adopting this practice, the start-up has fostered a collaborative environment where seasoned employees guide newcomers, enhancing creativity and efficiency. This approach not only expedites product development but also cultivates a culture of continuous learning, allowing for innovative solutions to emerge swiftly.

Global NGOs, too, have benefited from incorporating African leadership styles, particularly through community-led initiatives. For instance, when NGOs engage local communities in the planning and execution of programs, they witness increased effectiveness and volunteer participation. Community-led projects empower individuals by valuing their input and recognizing their unique insights into local challenges. This empowerment ensures that programs are tailored to address specific needs, hence improving delivery and outcomes. Volunteers working within such frameworks feel more invested in their roles, as they see their efforts directly contributing to meaningful changes within their communities.

Moreover, Multinational Corporations that have embraced African communal values report heightened employee satisfaction and retention rates. In a corporate setting where individuals often feel isolated or undervalued, the integration of communal principles creates a sense of belonging and purpose. African communal values emphasize collaboration, mutual respect, and shared success, fostering a workplace culture where employees feel supported and motivated. This result is a workforce that is more engaged and committed, reducing turnover and enhancing organizational stability.

To effectively replicate these successes, certain best practices should be considered. Organizations looking to integrate African leadership principles must first engage in cultural immersion and understanding. It is crucial to recognize the diversity across African cultures and identify which specific practices align with the organization's goals. Establishing partnerships with local leaders or advisors who are well-versed in these traditions can provide valuable insights and guidance.

Additionally, organizations should prioritize stakeholder engagement at all levels. African leadership thrives on inclusivity and dialogue, ensuring that voices from various segments of the community are heard and respected. Creating open channels of communication and collaborative platforms where ideas can be shared will facilitate smooth integration of these principles.

Flexibility in implementation is another key factor. While core values such as community orientation and mentorship remain consistent, their application might vary depending on the industry, location, and organizational structure. Being adaptable allows organizations to customize these principles to fit their specific context, enhancing their relevance and impact.

It is also important to continuously assess and evaluate the outcomes of implementing these practices. Regular feedback loops help organizations refine their approaches, celebrate successes, and address any challenges promptly. By doing so, they maintain momentum and ensure that the integration of African leadership principles remains sustainable over time.

Lessons Learned from These Success Stories

In exploring the successful implementation of African leadership practices in global businesses, several key insights emerge that can serve as actionable strategies for various business contexts. These insights are rooted firmly in collaborative efforts, culturally specific operations, mentorship programs, and diversity embracement—all of which have tangible impacts on problem-solving, stakeholder engagement, and competitive advantage.

Collaboration stands out as a powerful tool for boosting problem-solving capabilities and enhancing morale through community engagement. This approach thrives on the collective input of diverse team members. In many African leadership models, decision-making is communal, integrating input from all stakeholders to ensure comprehensive solutions. For instance, companies that encourage open dialogue and participatory problem-solving tend to innovate more effectively. By drawing from collective wisdom, businesses not only address complex challenges with creative solutions but also boost team morale. Employees feel valued, knowing their contributions influence significant decisions. This inclusive culture nurtures an environment where new ideas thrive because each member believes in their power to effect change.

Next, emphasizing cultural specificity in operations significantly enhances stakeholder connections and marketing strategies. Understanding and respecting the cultural dynamics within different regions or groups help organizations tailor their approaches more effectively. When businesses recognize unique cultural traits in their operations, they create meaningful relationships with stakeholders, leading to stronger brand loyalty and market penetration. Consider the example of a global fashion brand incorporating traditional African textiles and designs in their product lines, thereby resonating with local markets and fostering a sense of identification among consumers. This strategy acknowledges cultural nuances, allowing businesses to connect more deeply with their target audiences and differentiate themselves in competitive markets.

Mentorship programs become crucial in fostering competence and building generational partnerships, which result in competitive advantages through knowledge sharing. In traditional African settings, mentorship forms part of the social fabric, ensuring that skills and wisdom are passed down through generations. Transposing this to a modern business context, companies benefit immensely by establishing mentorship frameworks that encourage experienced professionals to guide less experienced colleagues. This dynamic not only enhances individual performance but also instills a culture of continuous learning and adaptation across the organization. Through mentorship, employees gain valuable insights they may not have encountered otherwise, preparing them to meet future challenges with confidence and creativity.

Embracing diversity is another cornerstone of effective leadership, promoting adaptability, resilience, and improved perceptions among stakeholders. Diverse teams bring varied perspectives to the table, enhancing creativity and innovation. Studies consistently show that organizations with diverse leadership teams outperform those without, primarily due to their ability to adapt quickly to changing environments and customer needs. Furthermore, diversity contributes to a positive corporate image, as companies perceived as inclusive often enjoy better reputations within the communities they serve. Encouraging diversity means actively recruiting individuals from different backgrounds, empowering them to share their unique voices, and creating spaces where differences are celebrated rather than suppressed.

The integration of these elements in business strategies results in compelling outcomes, driving success and proving the worth of African leadership principles in a global context. Companies embracing these strategies often report higher levels of employee engagement and satisfaction, leading to lower turnover rates and enhanced productivity. The alignment of business goals with these values ensures that organizations remain agile, ready to pivot strategies in response to evolving circumstances while maintaining strong connections with their stakeholders.

Final Insights

The chapter has thoroughly examined successful implementations of African leadership practices in global businesses, providing insightful examples that demonstrate their effectiveness. From the community-oriented decision-making of African Commodity Traders to the mentorship-fueled innovation at a Local Tech Start-up, these cases show how traditional African values can be integrated into modern business operations. By valuing trust and communal relationships, companies have fostered environments where creativity thrives and stakeholders feel genuinely included. The real-world outcomes highlighted include increased profitability, accelerated product development, and enhanced employee satisfaction, proving that these leadership models can drive sustainable growth and competitive advantage.

In adopting African leadership principles, global organizations are encouraged to immerse themselves in cultural understanding and prioritize inclusive stakeholder engagement. This flexibility in application, whether through community-led initiatives or the integration of communal values in corporate settings, has consistently led to improved organizational dynamics and success. The lessons learned emphasize the power of collaboration, cultural specificity, mentorship, and diversity, which collectively enhance problem-solving and stakeholder relations. As businesses aspire to replicate these successes, continuous evaluation and adaptation will ensure that the integration of these culturally rich practices remains impactful, paving the way for innovative and resilient business strategies worldwide.

Reference List

Galperin, B. L., Michaud, J., Betty Jane Punnett, Melyoki, L. L., Elham Metwally, Clive Mukanzi, Thomas Anyanje Senaji, & Taleb, A. (2024, June 1). *Towards Increased Understanding of Leadership in the African Context: Data From Seven Countries.* Journal of International Management; Elsevier BV. https://doi.org/10.1016/j.intman.2024.101170

McKinsey & Company. (2023, December 5). *Diversity matters even more: The case for holistic impact.* Www.mckinsey.com. https://www.mckinsey.com/featured-insights/diversity-and-inclusion/diversity-matters-even-more-the-case-for-holistic-impact

Nicolaides, A., & Tornam Duho, K. C. (2019). *Effective Leadership in Organizations: African Ethics and Corruption.* Modern Economy. https://doi.org/10.4236/me.2019.107111

psicosmart.net. (2019). *Case Studies: Successful Implementation of Cultural Diversity Management Solutions in Various Industries.* Psicosmart.net. https://psicosmart.net/blogs/blog-case-studies-successful-implementation-of-cultural-diversity-management-solutions-in-various-industries-173796

Leadership and Innovation

Leadership and innovation are deeply interconnected concepts that reflect a dynamic approach to shaping future pathways across various sectors. Exploring these themes within the context of African leadership offers unique insights into how communal creativity, intergenerational collaboration, and the balance between tradition and technology can serve as powerful catalysts for change. These elements not only shape individual communities but also impact global perspectives on effective leadership strategies. At the heart of this exploration lies an appreciation for diverse, non-Western methodologies, which challenge conventional norms and introduce rich cultural dimensions into the discourse on innovation and leadership. By examining the intricate relationships within African societies, one discovers the potential for transformative solutions grounded in heritage yet responsive to modern demands.

In this chapter, readers will delve into the ways African leadership principles foster environments ripe for innovation through a collective framework. The narrative unfolds by highlighting how communal practices nurture creative thinking and encourage collaborative problem-solving. It examines real-world examples from agricultural and technological spheres, illustrating how community-led initiatives have driven both local and regional advancements. Additionally, the chapter provides insight into the synergy between generations, showcasing how elders' wisdom complements the youthful energy of emerging leaders. By weaving together traditional practices with contemporary technologies, these discussions reveal a model for sustainable growth and cultural preservation. Ultimately, this chapter invites business leaders, academics, and entrepreneurs alike to consider how embracing communal values and diverse talents can enhance leadership effectiveness and drive innovative progress.

Encouraging Creativity within a Communal Framework

In the realm of African leadership, communal settings play a vital role in fostering creativity and driving innovative solutions. By nurturing an environment where inclusivity and collaboration are prioritized, African cultures have sculpted unique approaches that encourage creative thinking. Many African cultures utilize rituals that promote collective brainstorming sessions. These gatherings often bring together individuals from diverse backgrounds, enabling them to contribute their perspectives and insights. Such practices are not merely traditional ceremonies but structured environments designed to stimulate ideas and develop solutions that benefit the community as a whole.

Recognizing the talents of each community member is another fundamental aspect of these communal practices. This recognition fosters an atmosphere of inclusivity, ensuring everyone feels valued and heard. It's about identifying and celebrating the unique skills and knowledge that each person brings to the table. By doing so, these communities create a culture where innovation becomes a collective effort rather than an individual pursuit. In this setting, every voice matters, and every idea can potentially spark a breakthrough.

Case studies across various sectors illustrate how communal brainstorming significantly enhances creativity. For example, in agricultural communities, local farmers gather to share knowledge on sustainable practices, leading to improved crop yields and more efficient resource management. Similarly, technology startups in urban areas host regular hackathons, drawing from the collaborative spirit of these cultural traditions, which leads to the development of products that are both innovative and culturally relevant. In both scenarios, communal brainstorming sessions improve the quality of ideas generated, ultimately enhancing both product innovation and team dynamics.

The success of team-based projects within these communal frameworks lies in their ability to merge diverse insights. When individuals work together, they bring different perspectives and expertise, creating a rich tapestry of knowledge that fosters creativity. Collaborative ownership of projects encourages members to invest in the outcomes, reducing the fear of failure and promoting experimentation. This environment, where risk-taking is embraced and failures are viewed as learning opportunities, drives innovation forward.

Incorporating guidelines to foster the recognition of diverse talent within these settings can enhance their effectiveness. One approach is to establish platforms that highlight individual achievements and contributions, whether through storytelling events or recognition programs. These initiatives can provide individuals with the confidence to share their ideas and participate actively in communal efforts, thereby enriching the pool of creative resources available.

Encouraging collaborative projects further nurtures a culture of innovation. It is essential to create frameworks that allow for flexibility and adaptability. Teams should be encouraged to test new ideas without the fear of repercussion, promoting an open-minded approach to problem-solving. By structuring projects around clear objectives while allowing room for creativity, communities can achieve remarkable results that reflect the synergy of combined efforts.

In essence, communal settings within African cultures offer invaluable lessons in nurturing creativity to drive innovation. Through rituals that promote collective brainstorming, the recognition of diverse talents, case studies highlighting successful approaches, and the encouragement of collaborative projects, these communities demonstrate the power of unity in generating impactful solutions. Business leaders and managers seeking to enhance their leadership effectiveness can draw significant inspiration from these practices, integrating them into modern business strategies to foster an environment conducive to innovative thinking.

Intergenerational Knowledge Synergy and Balancing Tradition with Technology

In exploring the interplay between elders and youth within African leadership principles, it becomes evident that their dynamic serves as a catalyst for innovation. This symbiotic relationship hinges on harnessing the collective strengths of both groups, namely the wisdom of elders and the forward-thinking perspectives of the youth, to create a robust platform for continuous learning and mentorship.

Elders possess a vast repository of knowledge and experience, having navigated myriad challenges over the years. Their insights often stem from practical encounters with cultural, social, and economic issues that have shaped them into community pillars. By integrating this wisdom with the modern viewpoints of the youth, a comprehensive approach to problem-solving emerges. The youth, often more attuned to current trends and technologies, bring a fresh lens through which traditional methods can be reevaluated and improved upon. This blend of old and new perspectives lays down a strong foundation for fostering sustained growth and adaptability in an ever-evolving world.

Young leaders play a pivotal role in this innovative ecosystem. Their willingness to take risks and challenge established norms paves the way for groundbreaking initiatives. With a propensity to embrace digital tools and platforms, they spearhead efforts that are not only innovative but also resonate with contemporary societal needs. For instance, Africa has seen a surge in tech hubs led by young entrepreneurs who design solutions tailored to local challenges. These initiatives exemplify how youthful energy, when supported by elder guidance, can translate into tangible advancements in sectors such as agriculture, healthcare, and education.

To facilitate such generational exchanges, collaborative platforms become essential. These spaces—whether physical or virtual—allow for the sharing of insights in a manner that cultivates mutual respect. Such environments encourage dialogue, where elders' experiences can inform strategic decisions while the youth's enthusiasm injects vigor into operational processes. Programs like intergenerational mentorship schemes underscore the value of creating structured opportunities for these interactions. Here, the focus is on joint projects that marry tradition with modernity, thereby producing culturally relevant solutions that honor heritage while meeting present-day demands.

A prime example is seen in various indigenous communities where technology is used to preserve traditions. Digital storytelling projects, for instance, document oral histories and cultural artifacts, ensuring that they endure for future generations. By incorporating technological advancements, such initiatives gain wider acceptance and accessibility, broadening their impact beyond immediate geographical confines. The application of modern tools to safeguard historical richness underscores how traditions can be harmonized with technology to foster innovation.

Understanding the value of diverse insights requires acknowledging each participant's unique contributions. In age-diverse teams, as highlighted by Gerhardt et al. (2022), the juxtaposition of seasoned wisdom and youthful curiosity breeds environments ripe for creative breakthroughs. Acknowledging and valuing these differences enriches collaborative efforts, leading to improved decision-making and solutions that would otherwise elude homogeneous groups.

Guidelines for cultivating an intergenerational dialogue are crucial in maximizing these interactions. It begins with establishing systems that prioritize equal voice and participation, ensuring that no single perspective dominates the discourse. By setting clear expectations for mutual respect and open-mindedness, organizations can negate potential generational biases that might hinder cooperation. Moreover, assigning roles based on expertise rather than age further reinforces the notion of capability-driven contribution. This approach dismantles stereotypes and opens avenues for authentic engagement, making innovation a shared endeavor.

For businesses aiming to leverage these intergenerational dynamics, adopting inclusive practices is essential. Encouraging cross-generational mentorship, as seen in programs like reverse mentoring, where younger employees teach older colleagues about emerging technologies, fosters a culture of continuous learning and evolution. These practices not only enhance team dynamics but also align with broader diversity and inclusion objectives, propelling organizations toward sustainable growth.

Integrating traditional practices with contemporary technologies forms another cornerstone of innovative leadership. This synthesis ensures that advancements are rooted in cultural relevance, providing them with a foundation that resonates with wider audiences. When traditional agricultural techniques, for instance, are augmented with precision farming technologies, the result is often increased productivity and efficiency without diluting cultural identity. Such practices highlight the importance of contextually sensitive innovations that capitalize on existing knowledge while embracing new methodologies.

By embedding tradition within the framework of technological progress, there emerges a dual benefit: preserving cultural legacies while expanding reach and impact through modern means. This approach secures buy-in from stakeholders who may otherwise be wary of change, thereby facilitating smoother transitions and adoption of new strategies.

Concluding Thoughts

Throughout this chapter, we have explored the profound impact that African leadership principles can have on fostering innovation through communal creativity and intergenerational collaboration. By delving into how these communities emphasize inclusivity and collective effort, we've seen the unique approaches that emerge when diverse groups engage in shared problem-solving. Recognizing individual talents within a community amplifies creative potential, transforming innovation into a collective pursuit. The success stories from various sectors demonstrate that when different perspectives merge, the outcomes are enriched, reflecting both the cultural relevance and practical benefits of collaborative innovation.

Moreover, the interplay between elders and youth within these frameworks underscores the importance of balancing tradition with modernity. Elders provide invaluable wisdom derived from experience, while the younger generation offers fresh insights powered by emerging technologies. Together, they form an innovative ecosystem capable of addressing current challenges with depth and adaptability. This synergy is further enhanced by structured environments that facilitate dialogue and mutual respect, ultimately producing solutions that honor heritage while embracing progress. In integrating these principles, business leaders, students, and entrepreneurs alike can find inspiration to create environments where innovative thinking thrives, grounded in the rich tapestry of African communal practices and intergenerational collaboration.

Reference List

Gerhardt, M. W., Nachemson-Ekwall, J., & Fogel, B. (2022, March 8). *Harnessing the Power of Age Diversity*. Harvard Business Review. https://hbr.org/2022/03/harnessing-the-power-of-age-diversity

Native Youth and Culture Fund | First Nations Development Institute. (2017). Firstnations.org. https://www.firstnations.org/projects/native-youth-and-culture-fund/

Paulus, P. B., & Nijstad, B. A. (2003, September 25). *Group Creativity.* Group Creativity: Innovation through Collaboration. https://doi.org/10.1093/acprof:oso/9780195147308.001.0001

Sawyer, R. K., & Henriksen, D. (2023, December 14). *Culture and Creativity.* Oxford University Press EBooks; Oxford University Press. https://doi.org/10.1093/oso/9780197747537.003.0014

Cultural Heritage and Modern Business

Utilizing Africa's cultural heritage as a competitive asset in business is an endeavor that bridges the rich past with modern ambition. The interplay of cultural narratives and contemporary business practices offers a reservoir of untapped potential, presenting unique opportunities for organizations willing to explore this intersection. Africa's diverse traditions and stories can provide businesses with a distinct identity, one that resonates deeply with consumers seeking authenticity and connections beyond mere transactions. This chapter delves into how integrating these elements not only enhances brand storytelling but also fosters emotional engagement, driving customer loyalty and trust.

Throughout the chapter, readers will explore various strategies for leveraging African cultural heritage as a business advantage. Key topics include the power of storytelling within branding, where traditional folklore and community legends become pivotal tools in creating compelling brand identities. The chapter will also discuss the creation of culturally inspired products, highlighting how these offerings can appeal to both niche markets and international audiences looking for authentic representation. Additionally, cross-cultural marketing strategies will be examined, emphasizing the importance of aligning campaigns with diverse values and customs to reach broader audiences. Integrating cultural heritage into corporate social responsibility initiatives will be addressed, showcasing how companies can strengthen local ties and enhance their reputations through genuine community involvement. By the end of the chapter, readers will gain insights into the practical application of these concepts, equipping them with actionable steps to harness cultural heritage as a sustainable competitive edge in the business landscape.

Celebrating Cultural Diversity in the Workplace

Embracing cultural diversity within the corporate landscape is not just an ethical imperative; it is a strategic advantage that fosters innovation and enhances effectiveness in the workplace. The richness of varied cultural backgrounds can significantly contribute to creating a dynamic, inclusive environment that thrives on mutual respect and understanding among employees. By valuing these diverse perspectives, companies can unlock new levels of creativity and performance that are essential in today's competitive business world.

To begin with, creating an inclusive workplace involves more than simply hiring individuals from various backgrounds—it's about fostering an environment where every employee feels valued and respected for their unique contributions. This inclusion leads to greater mutual respect and understanding among team members, reducing conflicts and increasing collaboration. Employees who feel that their cultural identities are acknowledged are more likely to engage fully and contribute innovative ideas, propelling the organization towards success (Wong, 2024). Such environments nurture creativity as diverse cultural insights provide a pool of ideas from which the best solutions often emerge.

Implementing training programs focused on cultural awareness is another effective tool in promoting a harmonious work environment. These programs educate employees about different cultural norms and values, encouraging them to appreciate each other's unique backgrounds. Such training breaks down barriers, dispels stereotypes, and reduces unconscious biases that may hinder teamwork. When employees understand and embrace their colleagues' diverse backgrounds, they are more likely to collaborate effectively, share knowledge, and support one another. Training sessions can include interactive workshops, cultural competency courses, and immersive experiences designed to expand employees' horizons and deepen their empathy.

Leadership plays a crucial role in shaping a company's culture, and ensuring that leadership reflects the workforce's cultural diversity is vital. Diverse leadership teams bring a range of perspectives and experiences, enriching decision-making processes and providing insights that resonate with a broader audience. Leaders from diverse backgrounds can offer unique viewpoints that help in navigating complex challenges, crafting strategies that appeal to diverse markets, and driving innovation. Moreover, when employees see themselves represented in leadership positions, it boosts morale and motivates them to reach their full potential. Representation in leadership not only strengthens the organizational structure but also reinforces the message that every voice matters and everyone has the opportunity to succeed.

Organizing events that celebrate various cultures is another powerful way to promote inclusivity and team spirit. Cultural celebrations can take many forms, such as multicultural festivals, international food fairs, or themed events recognizing significant cultural holidays. These gatherings provide opportunities for employees to share their traditions, stories, and customs, fostering a sense of belonging and unity. Celebratory events not only enhance camaraderie but also encourage curiosity and learning among employees, broadening their understanding of global cultures and perspectives. Through these shared experiences, teams become more cohesive, leading to improved collaboration and communication.

Promoting inclusivity is not just a matter of policies and procedures; it requires genuine commitment and action from all levels within an organization. A guideline for promoting inclusivity can involve developing policies that prioritize equitable treatment, providing ongoing diversity training, and actively recruiting diverse talent to ensure representation at all levels of the company. Creating a safe space for open dialogues and encouraging feedback from employees about their inclusion experiences can also be instrumental. Such efforts demonstrate an organization's dedication to building an inclusive culture where every individual feels welcomed and valued.

Incorporating cultural awareness training into professional development initiatives is essential for equipping employees with the skills needed to navigate a multicultural workplace effectively. Guidelines for cultural awareness training should include educating staff on cultural nuances, communication styles, and conflict resolution strategies that consider diverse perspectives. Role-playing exercises and real-world scenarios can also be part of the training program, allowing employees to practice empathy and adaptability in a controlled environment. These guidelines ensure that cultural awareness becomes ingrained in the company's fabric, ultimately benefiting both the organization and its workforce by enhancing productivity and innovation.

Diverse leadership representation is a critical component of an inclusive workplace strategy. To achieve this, organizations should establish guidelines that focus on mentoring and supporting underrepresented groups in their journey to leadership roles. Succession planning should emphasize diversity, with clear pathways for advancement based on merit and potential rather than traditional network-driven promotions. Companies can set measurable diversity goals and hold leadership accountable for progress toward these objectives, ensuring that the composition of leadership mirrors the diversity within the broader workforce.

Celebrating cultural events with employee participation should be approached thoughtfully and respectfully. Guidelines here could include forming cross-departmental committees to plan and execute events, ensuring diverse cultural representation, and soliciting input from employees about which cultural traditions they'd like to celebrate. It's crucial to approach these celebrations with authenticity and sensitivity, avoiding tokenism and genuinely honoring the richness of the cultures represented within the organization. Employees should be encouraged to share their cultural stories and experiences through presentations, performances, or storytelling, facilitating deeper connections and understanding.

Leveraging Cultural Heritage for Competitive Advantage

In today's competitive business landscape, leveraging Africa's rich cultural heritage can be a powerful tool for differentiation and success. By incorporating cultural narratives into branding, businesses can create unique identities that resonate deeply with consumers. This approach allows companies to stand out in the crowded marketplace by offering something more than just a product—a story, an experience, and a connection that consumers can't find elsewhere.

Take, for instance, the power of storytelling in branding. When businesses incorporate cultural narratives, they are not just selling a product; they are telling a story. These stories can be drawn from historical events, traditional folklore, or community legends. By weaving these elements into their brand, businesses can forge authentic connections with their customers. For example, using African proverbs or symbols in marketing materials can evoke a sense of authenticity and pride, drawing customers who identify with those cultural aspects. This emotional engagement is crucial as it fosters brand loyalty and trust.

Developing culturally inspired products is another strategic advantage. Products that embrace cultural aesthetics, techniques, or traditions appeal to niche markets that value authenticity and originality. For example, a fashion brand might use traditional African textiles, known for their vibrant colors and intricate patterns, to develop a new clothing line. This approach not only caters to consumers looking for genuine cultural representation but also opens up opportunities in new markets abroad, where such products are perceived as exotic and desirable. The key is to respect and authentically integrate cultural elements, ensuring that they are not merely superficial additions, but integral parts of the product's identity.

Implementing cross-cultural marketing strategies can further extend a business's reach. This means aligning marketing efforts with the values and customs of diverse cultural groups, allowing businesses to connect on a deeper level with international audiences. Cross-cultural marketing requires a profound understanding of various cultures' values, beliefs, and communication styles. For example, a company targeting both Western and African markets might craft campaigns that highlight universal themes of family and community, which hold significance across different cultures. Moreover, by employing multilingual advertising and culturally nuanced content, businesses can foster inclusivity and broaden their appeal, reaching untapped customer bases and driving growth.

Integrating cultural heritage in corporate social responsibility (CSR) initiatives is equally impactful for reinforcing a company's brand authenticity. Businesses can engage in community projects that honor and preserve cultural traditions, thereby strengthening local ties and enhancing their reputation. For example, sponsoring cultural festivals, partnering with local artisans, or investing in heritage conservation projects demonstrates a commitment to community well-being and cultural preservation. This not only boosts the company's image but also encourages community support and pride in the brand. Involving employees and stakeholders in these initiatives can further cement the relationship between the company and its cultural roots, fostering a culture of respect and mutual benefits.

Moreover, culturally inspired products should not just aim for aesthetic appeal but also reflect the values and craftsmanship of the heritage they represent. For businesses venturing into this domain, a guideline could involve engaging with local artisans and communities to ensure the authenticity and fair representation of cultural elements. This collaboration can lead to innovations that maintain traditional art forms while adapting them for contemporary consumer needs, thus achieving both cultural preservation and market differentiation.

Similarly, implementing cross-cultural marketing strategies necessitates guidelines focused on cultural competence and sensitivity. Businesses should invest in understanding the cultural dynamics of their target markets through research and collaboration with cultural experts. Training sessions on cultural awareness for marketing teams can help avoid missteps and build campaigns that genuinely resonate with diverse audiences. An effective strategy involves tailoring messages that align with cultural values and using appropriate channels to engage different communities, thereby gaining their trust and fostering long-term loyalty.

Incorporating cultural heritage elements into CSR initiatives requires careful planning and alignment with the company's core values and mission. A guideline for businesses could include conducting thorough assessments to identify cultural needs within the community and designing programs that address those needs while promoting sustainability and heritage appreciation. Collaborating with local leaders and cultural custodians ensures that the initiatives are well-received and make a meaningful impact.

By thoughtfully integrating cultural heritage into various facets of business operations, companies can not only differentiate themselves in a saturated market but also contribute to the preservation and celebration of cultural identities. Embracing this approach enriches brand narratives, cultivates loyal customer bases, and positions businesses as culturally competent leaders in the global marketplace.

Final Insights

The chapter has explored how embracing Africa's cultural heritage can serve as a powerful tool for businesses looking to differentiate themselves in the marketplace. By weaving cultural narratives into branding, companies can create unique identities that resonate deeply with consumers. This strategy not only involves selling products but also telling stories that evoke emotional connections and foster brand loyalty. Aligning marketing efforts with the values and customs of diverse cultural groups allows businesses to connect on a deeper level with their audience, expanding their appeal and driving growth.

Additionally, integrating cultural elements into corporate social responsibility initiatives strengthens business-community ties and enhances brand authenticity. Engaging in projects that honor and preserve cultural traditions demonstrates a commitment to community well-being and promotes sustainable practices. By valuing local craftsmanship and collaborating with artisans, businesses can innovate while respecting and preserving cultural traditions. These approaches not only position companies as cultural leaders but also contribute to the celebration and preservation of African heritage, ultimately enriching brand narratives and cultivating dedicated customer bases.

Reference List

Heritage, C. (2018). *Leveraging Cultural Heritage For Branding And Marketing - FasterCapital.* FasterCapital. https://fastercapital.com/topics/leveraging-cultural-heritage-for-branding-and-marketing.html/1

Mediaculture. (2024). *The Crucial Role of Multicultural Marketing | Media Culture.* Www.mediaculture.com. https://www.mediaculture.com/multicultural-marketing

Penn LPS. (2023, March 22). *DEI in the workplace: Why It's Important for Company Culture | Penn LPS Online.* Lpsonline.sas.upenn.edu. https://lpsonline.sas.upenn.edu/features/dei-workplace-why-its-important-company-culture

Wong, K. (2024, March 25). *Diversity and inclusion in the workplace: Benefits and challenges.* Achievers. https://www.achievers.com/blog/diversity-and-inclusion/

Practical Strategies for Leaders

Leadership effectiveness is increasingly being understood through the lens of cultural diversity, with African principles offering valuable insights into building strong, principled leaders. More than ever, organizations are recognizing the importance of integrating these rich traditions and heritage into their leadership frameworks. The concepts originating from African cultural contexts provide a framework that emphasizes the significance of mentorship, community-driven strategies, and ethical decision-making. These elements serve as foundational pillars in crafting leaders who are not only competent but also deeply rooted in moral values, setting a new standard for leadership that values communal growth over individual accomplishments.

This chapter delves into various actionable strategies that leaders can adopt to enhance their effectiveness by embracing African leadership principles. Readers will explore the historical and cultural underpinnings of mentorship within African societies and learn how these practices can be adapted to modern organizational needs. The chapter examines different mentorship models, such as the renowned apprenticeship system, which has been instrumental in fostering entrepreneurship and economic growth across African regions like Nigeria. Furthermore, it discusses the significance of continuous learning and culturally informed leadership models in creating inclusive, dynamic work environments. With an emphasis on collective decision-making and community participation, this chapter provides leaders with practical tools to cultivate a culture of collaboration, innovation, and ethical leadership in their organizations. Through these insights, business leaders, students, and entrepreneurs alike will gain a deeper understanding of how integrating African principles can lead to sustainable organizational growth and a more inclusive workplace culture.

Implementing Mentorship and Culturally-Informed Leadership Models

Mentorship holds profound significance within African cultural contexts, shaping both personal and professional development. Traditional mentorship in African societies prioritizes growth through the transfer of ethical values vital for leadership. This approach underscores the importance of mentoring relationships based on mutual respect, integrity, and responsibility—qualities essential to nurturing future leaders who are not merely skilled but principled.

These timeless values anchor leadership effectiveness, ensuring that emerging leaders possess a strong moral compass to guide their decision-making processes. By emphasizing these ethical underpinnings, mentorship becomes a bridge connecting generations, allowing wisdom to flow seamlessly from one leader to another.

The apprenticeship model, renowned in various African societies, embodies an effective learning strategy that modern organizations can adopt. Rooted in cultural tradition, this hands-on learning experience encourages skill retention while perpetuating cultural practices. For example, the Igbo apprenticeship system in Nigeria exemplifies this by valuing practical training and community engagement, which have been crucial in developing entrepreneurial skills and fostering economic growth. This approach, supported by robust social networks, helps instill hard work and entrepreneurship values (The Igbo Apprenticeship System: A Model for Sustainable Entrepreneurship – Fordax Business School, 2023). Structuring contemporary apprenticeship programs based on similar principles could allow institutions to benefit from enhanced employee engagement and proficiency.

Incorporating African leadership principles into organizational frameworks ensures authenticity and resonance with diverse cultural backgrounds. At the core of these principles is the value placed on communal participation over individualistic pursuits. Emphasizing collective decision-making nurtures an environment where ideas are shared freely, leading to innovative solutions that reflect the group's consensus. This practice not only fosters collaboration but also imbues a sense of ownership among team members, as decisions result from inclusive dialogue rather than hierarchical mandates. Such collaborative environments mirror traditional African leadership structures, where elders convene to deliberate and reach agreements benefiting the broader community.

Embracing a continuous learning approach in mentorship programs facilitates dynamic adaptation to evolving cultural dynamics. Workshops, seminars, and ongoing mentoring relationships serve as educational avenues that address contemporary challenges while honoring traditional customs. These platforms offer opportunities for exchanging insights across generations, ensuring that newer practices align with longstanding cultural tenets. By fostering a culture of lifelong learning, organizations can remain agile and responsive, adapting practices to incorporate new knowledge while respecting historical foundations. Regular engagements also support skill reinforcement, enabling participants to hone capabilities crucial for maintaining competitive advantage in an ever-changing landscape.

As mentorship practices evolve, integrating African cultural elements enhances their relevance and effectiveness. Organizations must consider establishing guidelines to balance traditional methods with contemporary business needs. For instance, adopting a structured mentorship framework that outlines objectives, expectations, and periodic evaluations could help align traditional wisdom with modern organizational goals.

Creating Inclusive Work Environments Based on African Principles

To foster inclusive work environments, leaders can draw significantly from African communal values, particularly the Ubuntu philosophy. Ubuntu, often summarized as "I am because we are," emphasizes interconnectedness, respect, and compassion within a community. This principle dovetails seamlessly with modern organizational aspirations of inclusivity, offering a framework that celebrates diversity and fosters employee engagement.

Understanding Inclusivity in Context begins with exploring Ubuntu's ethos of togetherness and mutual respect. Unlike individual-centric leadership models predominantly seen in Western cultures, Ubuntu promotes a collective identity where shared goals and mutual support are paramount. This approach creates a level playing field for all employees, nurturing an atmosphere where every individual feels valued and heard. Inclusivity, therefore, is not just a policy but a deeply ingrained cultural dynamic, encouraging workplaces to look beyond transactional interactions to forge meaningful relationships across diverse backgrounds (Chetty & Price, 2024).

Connected to this understanding are Strategies for Inclusivity. Leaders can employ practical approaches like participatory decision-making, which mirrors traditional African councils where each community member has a voice. Encouraging teams to collaboratively deliberate and decide on matters enhances buy-in and satisfaction. Another strategy is the incorporation of team-building exercises designed to celebrate cultural diversities, thereby sparking innovation through diverse perspectives. Such practices not only harness creativity but also cultivate a vibrant organizational culture that thrives on collective achievements rather than individual accolades.

Additionally, Feedback Mechanisms play a pivotal role in enhancing organizational effectiveness. Establishing platforms for honest feedback aligns with Ubuntu's core values of openness and sincerity. Regular check-ins provide employees with opportunities to share insights about their experiences and propose improvements. Anonymous surveys or open forums can offer valuable data, allowing organizations to adapt and stay attuned to the needs and concerns of their workforce. Embracing these feedback loops ensures that workplace policies remain dynamic and employee-centered, boosting engagement by demonstrating a genuine commitment to addressing team concerns.

Case Studies of Success further illustrate how organizations successfully implementing inclusion strategies have reported remarkable results in employee satisfaction and productivity. South African tech company Dimension Data, for instance, has seen notable success by integrating Ubuntu principles into its management style. By prioritizing empathy and collective problem-solving, the company was able to enhance team cohesion and drive innovation. Similarly, the multinational firm Unilever, operating in diverse African markets, adopted African-inspired leadership frameworks, which led to improved cultural adaptability and local market relevancy. These examples underscore the transformative potential of culturally informed approaches to leadership, proving that an investment in people-oriented practices reaps substantial organizational benefits.

Bringing It All Together

Throughout this chapter, we have explored the profound impact of integrating African principles into leadership practices to enhance organizational effectiveness. By examining mentorship and culturally-informed leadership models, it is evident that incorporating traditional African values fosters the development of principled leaders who possess a strong moral compass. The apprenticeship model, deeply rooted in African culture, offers a dynamic learning strategy that organizations can adopt to strengthen skill retention and cultural continuity. These methods emphasize the value of collective participation, encouraging collaboration and shared ownership, which are essential for fostering an inclusive and innovative work environment.

As we conclude, it becomes clear that by embracing these concepts, organizations not only honor diverse cultural backgrounds but also create more effective and harmonious workplaces. Leaders who adopt Ubuntu's philosophy of interconnectedness and mutual respect can cultivate environments where all team members feel valued. Such leadership, centered on empathy and participatory decision-making, encourages open dialogue and adaptability, ensuring that both traditional wisdom and contemporary business needs are addressed. The case studies discussed offer powerful examples of how businesses can thrive by prioritizing community-driven leadership, illustrating the importance of investing in human-centered practices for sustainable success.

Reference List

Chetty, K., & Price, G. (2024, March 21). *Ubuntu leadership as a predictor of employee engagement: A South African study*. SA Journal of Human Resource Management.
https://doi.org/10.4102/sajhrm.v22i0.2462

Dei, D.-G. J. (2024, May 6). *Strategies for capturing, managing, and sharing indigenous knowledge*. Information Development.
https://doi.org/10.1177/02666669241248832

The Igbo Apprenticeship System: A Model for Sustainable Entrepreneurship – Fordax Business School. (2023, November 12). Fordaxbschool.com.
https://fordaxbschool.com/the-igbo-apprenticeship-system-a-model-for-sustainable-entrepreneurship/

Communal Leadership and Employee Engagement

Communal leadership is a pivotal element in cultivating a thriving workplace environment. It emphasizes the importance of viewing employees not merely as individuals, but as integral members of a community working toward shared objectives. This approach encourages a sense of belonging and unity, which can significantly increase motivation and productivity. By integrating communal values into leadership strategies, businesses can create a supportive atmosphere where employees are inspired to collaborate and contribute their best efforts. Such an environment not only enhances individual satisfaction but also drives collective success, fostering a vibrant organizational culture that stands out in today's competitive landscape.

This chapter delves into the dynamic relationship between communal leadership and employee engagement, exploring how inclusive practices build strong workplace connections. It examines various strategies for promoting a sense of community, such as organizing cultural events that unite employees through shared experiences and acknowledging individual contributions to encourage participation. Additionally, it discusses the design of inclusive workspaces that reflect corporate commitment to diversity and facilitate collaboration. By considering these elements, business leaders and managers can effectively engage their teams, creating environments where every member feels valued and heard. This narrative provides insights into leveraging community-oriented approaches to enhance employee engagement, ultimately leading to sustained organizational growth and success.

Promoting a Sense of Belonging in the Workplace

Creating a workplace culture that emphasizes belonging and community is crucial for enhancing employee engagement and overall organizational success. By fostering an environment where employees feel like they are part of a community, businesses can create spaces where individuals are motivated to contribute their best work. This sense of belonging not only boosts morale but also leads to higher productivity and innovation.

One effective way to enhance this feeling of belonging among employees is through engaging them in cultural events. These activities provide opportunities for employees to bond over shared experiences and build a collective identity within the organization. Cultural events, such as diversity celebrations, team-building exercises, or holiday gatherings, serve as touchpoints that connect employees on a personal level. They break down barriers and enable individuals from diverse backgrounds to come together, share their stories, and deepen their understanding of one another. When employees participate in these events, they are likely to develop stronger relationships with their colleagues, which contributes to a more cohesive and harmonious team dynamic.

Recognizing individual contributions is another critical aspect of building a strong workplace culture rooted in community values. When employees feel acknowledged and valued for their unique contributions, they are more inclined to bring their authentic selves to the workplace. Celebrating successes, both big and small, creates a sense of pride and ownership among employees. Such recognition can be manifested through awards, public acknowledgments during meetings, or personalized notes of appreciation. Recognizing individual contributions, whether through formal recognition programs or informal gestures, can act as a powerful motivator, boosting both morale and productivity. Additionally, when leaders highlight the strengths and achievements of each team member, it fosters an environment where diverse talents are celebrated, encouraging others to excel.

Inclusive workspace design is yet another way to reinforce community values within an organization.

Thoughtfully designed environments can physically manifest a company's commitment to inclusivity. Open-floor plans, accessible facilities, and communal areas encourage collaboration and create spaces where employees feel comfortable sharing their ideas. Inclusive designs also cater to various working styles, ensuring everyone has the opportunity to thrive in an environment that supports their needs. For instance, providing quiet zones for focused work while also having collaborative areas for group discussions reflects a balanced acknowledgment of different preferences and roles. This kind of layout not only increases comfort and accessibility but also reduces feelings of isolation, thus promoting a more inclusive and engaged workforce.

To further strengthen workplace community spirit, organizations should facilitate social interaction opportunities. Regular social activities, such as team lunches, coffee breaks, or retreats, allow employees to interact informally, building rapport outside of traditional work settings. These interactions help dismantle hierarchical boundaries, encouraging open communication and trust among team members. Social interactions foster a sense of belonging, as employees feel they are part of something greater than just their individual tasks. The bonds formed during these informal gatherings translate into improved teamwork and collaboration, as employees who understand and care for each other are more likely to support one another in professional endeavors. Consequently, fostering social interactions cultivates a vibrant and connected workplace, where communication flows easily and creativity flourishes.

In creating a workplace culture built on belonging and community, business leaders and managers must actively champion initiatives that prioritize inclusivity and engagement. This requires genuine commitment and effort to create a supportive environment where every employee feels valued and heard. Successful implementation of these practices involves listening to employees' needs, incorporating their feedback, and continuously evolving policies to reflect the diverse tapestry of the workforce. By doing so, organizations not only enhance employee satisfaction and retention but also unlock the full potential of their teams, leading to sustained growth and success.

The importance of cultivating a culture of belonging extends beyond immediate organizational benefits. Research has consistently shown that when employees experience a sense of belonging, they exhibit higher levels of job satisfaction, increased loyalty, and greater emotional investment in their roles (Bennett, 2024). This translates into tangible business outcomes, including heightened productivity, reduced turnover rates, and improved financial performance. Therefore, making belonging a strategic priority is not merely a matter of improving workplace morale; it is about driving substantial business results.

Fostering a community-oriented workplace culture also aligns with broader societal trends towards diversity, equity, and inclusion. As businesses increasingly recognize the value of diverse perspectives, they have the opportunity to become leaders in setting standards for inclusivity within their industries (Choice, 2024). By doing so, companies can leverage their commitment to belonging as a competitive advantage, attracting top talent and building a positive reputation among clients and stakeholders.

Utilizing Feedback Loops and Nurturing Multi-Generational Teams

In the modern workplace, engaging employees goes beyond mere policy; it requires a commitment to inclusivity and participation. A key component in this is involving employees in decision-making processes and embracing generational diversity. These practices not only enhance engagement but also foster a collaborative culture that values every team member's contribution.

Routine Feedback Mechanisms

Establishing routine feedback mechanisms enables continuous communication between management and staff. This practice promotes transparency and trust, essential elements for fostering an engaged workforce (Alshaabani et al., 2021). When employees feel their opinions are valued, they are more likely to invest energy into their work and strive for excellence. Regular feedback sessions should be structured to allow open dialogue, enabling employees to voice concerns and share ideas. For instance, weekly or monthly one-on-one meetings can be implemented to ensure individual attention and provide a platform for personal development discussions. By consistently seeking input, organizations can identify areas for improvement and recognize achievements, leading to enhanced job satisfaction and a stronger sense of belonging within the team.

Collaborative Decision-Making Processes

When employees participate in decision-making, they feel a deeper connection to the organization's goals and direction. Collaborative decision-making empowers individuals by giving them a stake in the outcomes, which fosters accountability and ownership. Additionally, diverse teams bring varied perspectives to the table, enriching the problem-solving process with innovative solutions. For example, forming cross-functional teams for project planning allows different departments to contribute their expertise, resulting in more comprehensive strategies. It is crucial, however, to ensure all voices are heard during discussions, creating an inclusive atmosphere where each opinion is respected. Organizations can utilize tools like democratic voting on major decisions or brainstorming sessions, where ideas are freely exchanged without judgment. This approach not only strengthens team cohesion but also improves the quality of decisions made, as they reflect a collective understanding of challenges and opportunities.

Mentorship Programs Across Generations

Mentorship programs serve as a bridge connecting older and younger employees, facilitating the exchange of knowledge and experiences. Such initiatives encourage inter-generational understanding, which is vital in today's diverse workforce. Younger employees benefit from the wisdom and guidance of seasoned professionals, gaining insights that may not be immediately apparent through formal training. Conversely, older employees can learn about new technologies and contemporary trends from their younger counterparts. To implement successful mentorship programs, companies should focus on pairing mentors and mentees based on shared interests and professional goals. Regularly scheduled interactions, whether in person or virtual, can ensure ongoing support and the development of strong professional relationships. As these connections grow, they help build a harmonious workplace culture where different generations feel appreciated and understood, which in turn supports organizational growth and innovation.

Creating Adaptable Roles

Recognizing and adapting to generational strengths and preferences is another critical aspect of enhancing employee engagement. By tailoring roles to align with individual capabilities and aspirations, organizations can boost morale and productivity. Flexible job descriptions that allow employees to take on new responsibilities or shift focus as needed can accommodate changing interests and career paths. Employers might offer options such as remote work, flexible hours, or part-time positions to better suit different life stages and personal commitments. For instance, providing opportunities for Gen Z employees to engage with technology-driven projects could leverage their digital native skills, while offering Boomers roles that emphasize mentorship and leadership could harness their wealth of experience. Such adaptability not only satisfies personal preferences but also nurtures respect and admiration among colleagues, reinforcing a sense of unity and purpose.

Implementing these strategies effectively requires a commitment to understanding the unique characteristics and needs of a multi-generational workforce. By actively involving employees in decision-making and creating an environment that values diversity, organizations can cultivate a culture of collaboration and mutual respect. This approach leads to higher levels of engagement, as employees see themselves as integral parts of the organization's success. Moreover, by investing in mentorship programs and adaptable roles, companies can ensure continuous learning and development, preparing their workforce for future challenges and opportunities.

Final Insights

In this chapter, we delved into the pivotal role of fostering a community-oriented workplace to boost employee engagement. We've discussed how creating an inclusive environment where employees feel valued and connected can dramatically enhance productivity and innovation. By participating in cultural events and recognizing individual contributions, organizations can cultivate a strong sense of belonging among their workforce. These practices not only break down barriers but also encourage individuals from diverse backgrounds to connect on a personal level, fostering deeper relationships and team cohesion.

Moreover, by designing inclusive workspaces and facilitating social interactions, organizations reinforce community values that make employees feel part of something larger than their individual roles. This approach leads to improved communication, collaboration, and overall job satisfaction. As businesses prioritize inclusivity and engagement, they remain aligned with broader societal shifts toward diversity, equity, and inclusion. By embracing these strategies, leaders and managers can ensure sustained growth and success while promoting a vibrant workplace culture where everyone feels heard and respected.

Reference List

Alshaabani, A., Hamza, K. A., & Rudnák, I. (2021, December 31). *Impact of Diversity Management on Employees' Engagement: The Role of Organizational Trust and Job Insecurity.* Sustainability; Researchgate. https://doi.org/10.3390/su14010420

Bridging the Generational Gap: Tailoring HR Strategies for Diverse Workforce Engagement - Transform. (2024, July 15). Transform. https://transform.us/articles/bridging-generational-gap-hr-strategies-workforce-engagement/

Bennett, A. (2024, February 23). *What is Workplace Belonging and Why is it Important?* The Diversity Movement. https://thediversitymovement.com/what-is-workplace-belonging-why-is-it-important/

Choice, E. (2024, June 10). *Embrace Cultural Diversity to Enhance Team Engagement*. Hppy. https://gethppy.com/employee-engagement/how-to-embrace-cultural-diversity-to-enhance-team-engagement

A Vision for the Future

Envisioning the future of global leadership requires us to look beyond traditional paradigms, embracing models that have long been overlooked yet possess remarkable transformative potential. African leadership philosophies provide a unique lens through which we can redefine what effective leadership means on a global scale. These philosophies, steeped in rich cultural traditions and practices, offer insights into how collective well-being and community-centered approaches can lead to more inclusive and sustainable leadership frameworks. By delving into these concepts, leaders can begin to see beyond the confines of individual success, shifting their focus towards shared goals that benefit the broader community and promote cross-cultural collaboration.

This chapter delves into how integrating African leadership models can reshape educational systems and business practices worldwide. It explores various philosophical insights like Ubuntu and decision-making processes such as the Igbo Council of Elders, highlighting their impact on fostering a culture of collaboration, consensus-building, and resilience. Readers will uncover the practical applications of these models, understanding how they can be incorporated into modern leadership strategies to address contemporary challenges. Through real-world examples and an exploration of cross-cultural dialogues, this chapter underscores the power of African leadership methodologies in bridging cultural gaps, fostering innovation, and creating environments where every member feels valued. As the narrative unfolds, it becomes evident how these paradigms not only align with but also enhance efforts towards sustainable growth and enriched organizational dynamics on a global level.

Implications for Global Leadership Paradigms

In a world increasingly interconnected by globalization, African leadership philosophies offer valuable insights that can transform global leadership models. These philosophies emphasize collaboration and community-centric approaches over individual accomplishments, fostering an inclusive understanding of what makes leadership effective. By examining these unique perspectives, we can begin to reorient leadership success towards a collective vision.

One critical aspect is the reimagining of leadership success. Traditional leadership often measures success by individual achievement and authority. In contrast, African leadership philosophies prioritize the well-being of the community. By emphasizing collective goals over personal ones, leaders can inspire cross-cultural collaboration and engagement. An example of this philosophy in action is the "Ubuntu" concept, embraced in many African cultures, which infers "I am because we are." This mindset encourages leaders to focus on group welfare, creating environments where every team member feels valued and integral to shared achievements (Ubuntusoul, 2024).

Integrating traditional wisdom into modern leadership practices provides alternative solutions to contemporary challenges. Traditional decision-making processes, such as the Igbo Council of Elders in Nigeria, bring cultural sensitivity and resilience to problem-solving. These councils leverage extensive local knowledge, prioritizing communal harmony and long-term benefits—a critical shift from short-term gains often pursued in Western models. By drawing on these robust decision-making frameworks, leaders can enhance their strategies with culturally sensitive and sustainable solutions. Incorporating traditional wisdom requires a deeper appreciation for diverse historical contexts, offering leaders a broader perspective and a toolkit grounded in cultural nuances, resulting in more effective and inclusive strategies.

Promoting holistic leadership recognizes the importance of emotional, social, and ethical dimensions. Such leadership goes beyond operational efficiency to consider the human aspects of organizational life. Leaders who embrace this approach foster a culture where employees feel connected and involved. Emotional intelligence, empathy, and ethical responsibility become cornerstones of leadership practice. This leads to deeper team engagement and increased employee loyalty, as seen in organizations that integrate compassionate leadership styles akin to those found in Ubuntu. Such practices ensure a work environment where trust and mutual respect thrive, fostering productivity and innovation.

Moreover, bridging the gap between cultures is essential in today's multicultural workplaces. By facilitating open dialogues between different cultural groups, leaders can encourage innovation and inclusivity. African leadership models stress the importance of valuing diverse perspectives, thus allowing global organizations to harness a variety of viewpoints. Kgotla meetings in Botswana serve as an excellent example of democratic decision-making processes that value consensus and inclusivity. By adopting similar practices, leaders can bridge cultural gaps, resulting in enriched communication and enhanced organizational cohesion.

This transformative potential also involves recognizing the importance of cooperative relationships over confrontational dynamics. Leaders influenced by African philosophies understand the power of collaboration. Rather than seeing conflict as a challenge, they view it as an opportunity for growth. They use participatory approaches to engage all stakeholders, ensuring that decisions are well-rounded and supported by those affected.

A guideline for integrating traditional leadership wisdom effectively involves creating space for dialogue and understanding within teams. Encourage members to share insights from their backgrounds and experiences, utilizing collective intelligence to inform decisions. Appreciate and respect cultural nuances and traditions in your organization, crafting policies and practices that resonate with diverse cultural values. Building partnerships with local communities can also provide a wealth of traditional knowledge, adding depth to organizational strategies. This integrative approach not only enriches leadership perspectives but also strengthens engagements with local and international partners.

Implementing these philosophies doesn't require abandoning existing models entirely but rather complementing them with richer, culturally-informed practices. Business leaders can craft new narratives of success by embracing a holistic view of leadership that prioritizes people and planet over profit. This transition includes a commitment to nurturing talent across borders, recognizing the universality yet uniqueness of leadership challenges worldwide.

As organizations strive for sustainability, it is crucial to rethink how leadership influences broader societal impacts. The global adoption of African leadership philosophies signifies not just adaptation to change but a conscious choice to create a future rooted in equity and shared prosperity. By learning from these time-tested models, contemporary leaders can navigate complex global dynamics with agility and foresight.

Driving Change in Business Schools and Curricula

In today's interconnected world, the integration of diverse leadership models into educational curricula has become crucial for fostering effective future leaders. The transformative potential of African leadership models presents a unique opportunity to enrich global paradigms and educational systems. By incorporating these models into the curriculum, educators can pave the way for leaders who are not only competent but also culturally aware and versatile.

One pivotal step in this direction is curricular innovation. Traditional business education often centers around Western leadership styles, which may not fully encapsulate the complexities and richness of global perspectives. African-rooted case studies can serve as practical examples, providing students with insights into leadership that values community, resilience, and adaptability. These case studies offer lessons in overcoming obstacles through collective effort and emphasize a holistic approach to problem-solving that can be particularly beneficial in today's complex business environments. For instance, showcasing how community-centric leadership in places like Ghana or Kenya fosters economic growth and social cohesion can broaden students' understanding of successful leadership dynamics beyond individualistic approaches.

Fostering cultural intelligence among students is another critical element in preparing them for global diversity. As leaders navigate multicultural workspaces, an understanding of various leadership styles becomes essential. African leadership models, with their focus on communalism and shared objectives, challenge the common notion of hierarchical decision-making. This exposure not only equips students to operate efficiently in diverse environments but also enhances their ability to negotiate and mediate across cultural lines. Introducing role-playing exercises based on African leadership scenarios can help students develop empathy and cultural sensitivity, skills that are invaluable in today's globalized economy.

Moreover, building global networks through partnerships with African institutions can significantly enrich student experiences. Such collaborations encourage knowledge exchange and provide firsthand exposure to alternative leadership frameworks. Universities might consider establishing exchange programs or collaborative research projects with African schools. These initiatives can enable students from different backgrounds to explore diverse leadership styles and cultivate international friendships and professional relationships. For example, engineering students from Nigeria and the United States working together on sustainable energy solutions could learn to appreciate each other's methodological approaches and jointly tackle global challenges.

Additionally, championing an inclusive leadership paradigm within educational institutions underscores the value of multiple leadership styles. This approach advocates for a shift in perspective, where leadership efficacy is measured by one's ability to adapt and integrate diverse strategies rather than conforming to a single model. Educational settings that endorse inclusivity often see positive results in their workforce, such as heightened employee engagement and broader talent retention. Business schools can lead this initiative by diversifying their curricula to include discussions on leadership models from all six continents, organizing guest lectures featuring African business leaders, and supporting student-led initiatives focused on inclusive leadership practices.

Integrating African leadership models into educational systems not only broadens the horizons of future leaders but also aligns with current educational trends emphasizing the need for a more globally conscious citizenry. As digitalization continues to reshape industries worldwide, leaders capable of thinking broadly, embracing change, and valuing diversity will likely excel. Programs integrating these elements prepare students to initiate impactful changes and drive innovative solutions in varied contexts.

Insights and Implications

The transformative potential of African leadership models on global paradigms and educational systems offers a new lens through which leaders can redefine success and foster inclusion. This chapter examines the shift from traditional leadership practices that prioritize individual achievement to those that emphasize community well-being. By embracing concepts such as Ubuntu, leaders are encouraged to create environments where collaboration and collective goals take precedence. These African philosophies not only enrich current leadership strategies but also align with the growing understanding that diverse perspectives and cultural sensitivity are vital for thriving in today's interconnected world.

Incorporating these insights into educational curricula is crucial for preparing future leaders who are culturally aware and adaptable. By integrating African-rooted case studies and fostering cultural intelligence, academic institutions can equip students with the skills necessary to navigate multicultural workspaces. Collaborative projects and partnerships with African institutions further enhance this experience, providing practical exposure to alternative leadership frameworks. Such educational innovations pave the way for inclusive and versatile leadership approaches, ensuring that the next generation of leaders is well-prepared to embrace diversity and drive positive change in various contexts.

Reference List

Research-Based Curriculum Review: Learning from the Africa Leadership Study – InSights Journal. (2014). Insightsjournal.org. https://insightsjournal.org/research-based-curriculum-review-learning-from-the-africa-leadership-study/

Ubuntusoul. (2024, June 5). *Ubuntu Philosophy and Leadership: Cultivating Community and Compassion.* Medium; Medium. https://medium.com/@ubuntusoul/ubuntu-philosophy-and-leadership-cultivating-community-and-compassion-d4d14c9f5ba7

Uleanya, C., & Naicker, S. R. (2024, March 27). *Future-fit and Innovative School Leadership in the*

African Context: Lesson for Sustainability in Underdeveloped and Developing Countries. Leadership and Policy in Schools. https://doi.org/10.1080/15700763.2024.2335618

Vandyck, C. K. (2023). *Embracing Indigenous Leadership Models for Africa's Development Renaissance – WACSI.* Wacsi.org. https://wacsi.org/embracing-indigenous-leadership-models-for-africas-development-renaissance/

Conclusion

African leadership principles are deeply woven into the fabric of many societies, embodying values that transcend time and geographical boundaries. As we delve into this chapter, we begin a journey to explore how these enduring values hold significance in today's ever-evolving world. African leadership is not merely a set of practices; it essentially forms a philosophy that echoes through various aspects of community life, emphasizing unity, empathy, and a shared vision. These core tenets offer more than just historical insight—they provide practical frameworks for addressing modern challenges across diverse fields. By examining the lessons embedded within these traditions, we open ourselves to the transformative potential they possess when applied to contemporary leadership settings. This exploration invites us to consider not only what has been but also what could be, using African leadership as a guiding beacon.

Within the richness of African leadership, this chapter navigates through key themes that illuminate its profound impact on modern practices. Through a narrative lens, we will uncover how concepts like community involvement, collaboration, and cultural intelligence can be revitalized and harnessed in today's professional environments. The essence of these principles, rooted in Ubuntu and communal decision-making, serves as a foundation for fostering inclusive and innovative workplaces. Readers will gain insights into the ways businesses have successfully integrated these methodologies, resulting in enhanced team dynamics and strategic growth. Furthermore, we will discuss how adopting such principles provides ethical frameworks vital for navigating complex global interactions. As we progress, the chapter offers practical examples and strategies, illustrating how leaders from diverse industries can incorporate these age-old beliefs to achieve tangible success and resilience. Through this examination, we aim to inspire a shift towards leadership that not only prioritizes profit but also upholds the dignity and connectedness of individuals within organizations and communities alike.

Summarizing Core Themes and Key Lessons

Reflecting upon the vast landscape of African leadership values, it's essential to recognize the profound wisdom embedded within these principles and their relevance in contemporary contexts. At the heart of African leadership lies a commitment to community, collaboration, and cultural intelligence. These foundational tenets serve as guiding lights in navigating both personal and professional landscapes worldwide.

African leadership is fundamentally about community. Considered the lifeblood of any substantial initiative, the idea of community goes beyond mere aggregation of individuals; it is about creating a sense of belonging and shared purpose. This principle can be seen throughout African societies where decisions are made collectively, ensuring that every voice is heard and valued. For business leaders, this translates into a team-centric approach, where success is a shared endeavor rather than an individual achievement. By fostering inclusive environments, leaders can draw out diverse perspectives, driving innovation and enhancing organizational resilience.

Collaboration is another cornerstone of African leadership values. In many African cultures, the concept of working together is ingrained from an early age. The story of the children who held hands and ran towards the sweets underpins this value — the realization that achievements are more meaningful when attained cooperatively. Modern leadership challenges, like managing complex global teams or resolving cross-cultural conflicts, can benefit substantially from this emphasis on collaboration. Leaders who encourage teamwork and mutual support are better positioned to harness collective strengths, leading to more effective problem-solving and creativity.

The third pillar, cultural intelligence, speaks to the ability to navigate and leverage cultural diversity with sensitivity. Africa's rich tapestry of languages, traditions, and customs requires leaders to develop an acute awareness of cultural nuances. This understanding is crucial in today's globalized world, where interactions span multiple cultures and backgrounds. Business leaders and managers gain a competitive edge by fostering a culture of inclusion and embracing diverse viewpoints. Cultural intelligence thus enables leaders to build more cohesive teams and strengthen international partnerships.

Ubuntu philosophy underscores and enriches these leadership values. Rooted in the belief of interconnectedness and shared humanity, Ubuntu teaches us that one's well-being is intrinsically linked to that of others. It's a call for empathy and compassion in leadership. Applying Ubuntu in global leadership contexts encourages a shift from a self-centered perspective to one where communal welfare is prioritized. Its implications are far-reaching as it inspires leaders to cultivate environments where empathy is practiced, and every individual's dignity is upheld. Consequently, organizations become spaces of mutual respect and inspiration, directly impacting employee morale and productivity.

To grasp how these values play out in practical terms, consider examples documented in various chapters of this book. Take, for instance, the transformation witnessed in companies that have embraced collaborative models inspired by African leadership concepts. Leaders in such organizations recognize that change management isn't solely about processes but about people coming together to achieve common goals. In another case, businesses employing cultural intelligence report greater success in expanding into new markets, demonstrating the tangible benefits of an inclusive approach to leadership.

Furthermore, the Ubuntu philosophy has been pivotal in reshaping leadership training programs globally. These programs incorporate African humanistic values, resulting in leaders who are not just strategic thinkers but also empathetic listeners and mentors. By integrating these principles, businesses foster leaders who are better equipped to handle ethical dilemmas, promote sustainability, and champion corporate responsibility.

Inspiring Future Actions and Vision

African leadership principles are rich in wisdom and deeply rooted in the communal and cultural ethos that have guided societies for generations. By encouraging the implementation of these insights today, we stand on the precipice of a transformative shift in both personal development and organizational dynamics. The core of these principles is to inspire action;

therefore, it becomes imperative for individuals to internalize these teachings in their daily interactions and decisions.

One of the most compelling aspects of African leadership practices is their ability to motivate and bring about meaningful change. Embracing values such as empathy, inclusivity, and cooperation can significantly enhance personal and professional relationships. By drawing inspiration from African leaders who prioritize community welfare over personal gain, readers can begin fostering environments where collaboration and mutual respect thrive. This shift not only enhances individual growth but also creates room for collective success.

Implementing communal leadership principles within organizational settings offers strategies that are adaptable across various industries. In business, this might manifest as creating more inclusive decision-making processes or developing policies that consider the diverse needs of all employees. Organizations could establish committees that reflect the community's diversity, ensuring that voices traditionally marginalized are heard and advocated for. Team leaders might encourage collaborative problem-solving workshops, where ideas are exchanged openly, fostering innovation and camaraderie. Managers should be encouraged to lead with empathy, recognizing and nurturing the unique strengths each team member brings. By emphasizing shared objectives over individual accolades, companies can cultivate a more united workforce poised for sustained success. Such environments not only increase job satisfaction but also drive productivity by weaving unity into the organizational fabric.

The global perspective on adopting African leadership methodologies reveals a promising transformation in how leadership paradigms are perceived and executed worldwide. As globalization continues to blur geographical boundaries, integrating these principles into international discourse could redefine how leaders approach governance and management. For instance, the principle of Ubuntu, which emphasizes human interconnectedness, could serve as a guiding framework for international collaborations, promoting peace and understanding between nations. In boardrooms across continents, adopting a mindset that prioritizes humanity over profit could result in more ethical and equitable business practices. Similarly, educational institutions globally might integrate African philosophies into curricula, preparing future leaders who are culturally intelligent and socially responsible. Such a global shift not only enhances cross-cultural communication but also aligns leadership practices with the evolving needs of an interconnected world.

Envisioning a future where African leadership principles guide societal changes opens up exciting possibilities for innovation and sustainable development. Consider a future where cities are designed with collective well-being in mind, harnessing local knowledge and traditions to create spaces that foster community interaction and environmental sustainability. Imagine governments that operate transparently and efficiently, inspired by leadership models that value accountability and public engagement. In this envisioned future, technology may be leveraged not just for economic growth but as a tool for enhancing social bonds and bridging gaps caused by inequality and division.

Additionally, the arts and culture sectors could flourish under African leadership philosophies, embracing diversity and creativity as catalysts for progress. Artistic expressions that celebrate cultural heritage and innovation may become conduits for dialogue and healing, allowing societies to navigate complex challenges with grace and resilience.

As we ponder these potential futures, it's crucial to recognize the importance of a supportive infrastructure that nurtures emerging leaders equipped with these transformative values. Investment in leadership development programs tailored to address contemporary challenges while respecting traditional wisdom will play a pivotal role in ensuring the continuity of these impacts. Universities and training institutes should incorporate modules focused on ethical leadership, community engagement, and conflict resolution, grounded in African thought systems. Governments and private sectors must collaborate to create pathways for young leaders from diverse backgrounds, enabling them to shape policies and initiatives that reflect inclusive and forward-thinking ideals.

Bringing It All Together

In this chapter, we delved into the rich tapestry of African leadership principles, emphasizing their foundational values of community, collaboration, and cultural intelligence. We explored how these tenets, rooted deeply in cultural ethos, can be applied to modern organizational frameworks to inspire growth, innovation, and inclusivity. By examining real-world examples and case studies, we highlighted how embracing these values enhances personal development and professional environments, making them more resilient and adaptive to change. Leaders inspired by African philosophies are better equipped to foster inclusive teams, harness diverse perspectives, and prioritize empathy over individual gain, resulting in cohesive and effective leadership.

As we reflect on these insights, it's clear that adopting African leadership principles presents a transformative opportunity for both individuals and organizations. By integrating ideas like Ubuntu into daily practices, we pave the way for a future where mutual respect and shared objectives drive success. Businesses and leaders who embrace these teachings can cultivate spaces where innovation thrives through collective effort, and meaningful connections flourish across cultural boundaries. This chapter has laid the groundwork for understanding how African leadership values not only benefit modern enterprises but also contribute to a more equitable and connected global society.

Reference List

Chanda, T. C., & Chitondo, L. (2024). *Leadership for sustainable development in Africa: A comprehensive perspective. International Journal of Research Publication and Reviews*, 5(2), 2395-2410. https://www.researchgate.net/publication/378365549_Leadership_for_Sustainable_Development_in_Africa_A_Comprehensive_Perspective

Ogechi Adeola. (2024, April 2). *Leveraging Ubuntu-inspired values to promote sustainable digital entrepreneurship in Africa*. Africa Journal of Management; Taylor & Francis. https://doi.org/10.1080/23322373.2024.2349484

Smita Raghum. (2024, January 28). *Is Ubuntu the Secret to Leadership Success? | Coacharya.* Coacharya. https://coacharya.com/blog/rethinking-power-is-ubuntu-the-leadership-game-changer/

Strinivasan Soondrasan Pillay, & Eustache Tanzala Kikasu. (2024, January 1). *Servant Leadership Style: A Key to Effective Good Governance and Sustainable Public Service Delivery in Africa.* Open Journal of Political Science; Bentham Science Publishers.
https://doi.org/10.4236/ojps.2024.141004